THE
INCREDIBLE
PAYBACK

THE INCREDIBLE PAYBACK

INNOVATIVE SOURCING SOLUTIONS
THAT DELIVER EXTRAORDINARY RESULTS

Dave Nelson

Patricia E. Moody

Jonathan R. Stegner

⁑AMACOM

American Management Association

New York * Atlanta * Brussels * Chicago * Mexico City
* San Francisco * Shanghai * Tokyo * Toronto * Washington, D.C.

Special discounts on bulk quantities of AMACOM books are available to corporations, professional associations, and other organizations. For details, contact Special Sales Department, AMACOM, a division of American Management Association, 1601 Broadway, New York, NY 10019.
Tel.: 212-903-8316. Fax: 212-903-8083.
Web site: www.amacombooks.org

This publication is designed to provide accurate and authoritative information in regard to the subject matter covered. It is sold with the understanding that the publisher is not engaged in rendering legal, accounting, or other professional service. If legal advice or other expert assistance is required, the services of a competent professional person should be sought.

Library of Congress Cataloging-in-Publication Data

Nelson, Dave, 1937–
    The incredible payback : innovative sourcing solutions that deliver extraordinary results / Dave Nelson, Patricia E. Moody, Jonathan R. Stegner.
        p. cm.
    Includes index.
    ISBN 0-8144-7207-9 (hardcover)
    1. Industrial procurement. 2. Purchasing. I. Moody, Patricia E. II. Stegner, Jonathan, 1954– III. Title.

    HD39.5.N455 2004
    658.7'2—dc22   2004006192

Printing number

'0 9 8 7 6 5 4 3 2 1

Dedication

For R. Gene Richter
Sept. 20, 1937 – July 28, 2003

When Gene Richter assumed the role of Chief Procurement Officer at IBM, he knew he was taking on a tough, stubborn challenge. However, he also knew that purchasing held the key to unlocking cash that IBM badly needed to attempt a turnaround. The naysayers were predicting that Big Blue would be divided up into a handful of Baby Blues—and that would have spelled the end of the giant's hold on technology and innovation. But Gene saw the possibilities, and he left a fun and comfortable position at Hewlett-Packard in California to return to the snows of upstate New York, and to save "a national treasure." It was an offer he could not refuse.

Gene was a giant in the supply chain world, a consummate professional known for his ethical and straightforward stance, the same generous and demanding guy in both his personal and his professional lives. His first training as a junior buyer at Ford was succeeded by every other purchasing position, but he always considered himself a buyer.

Gene was the only person to receive *Purchasing* magazine's Medal of Excellence three times in a row, first for Black and Decker, next for Hewlett-Packard, and finally for IBM. He understood the incredible payback and what it took to organize and staff a powerful supply management operation based on technology, the best of the best professionals, and spend management. By the time he retired from IBM, he had freed up $9 billion in cash, money that enabled the turnaround.

We much appreciated Gene's open and enthusiastic support of this book project, and we only wish he could have been here to receive the first copy off the presses.

Contents

Preface

Spend Management, the Twenty-First Best Practice

In tennis, the serve is the only stroke that can be completely controlled by the player—not the forehand, which can be loaded with an opponent's spin, not the backhand, which can be tough for many right-handed players, not the volley, not the lob, which puts good players in defensive positions. Only the serve will consistently put properly prepared players in the game, and allow them, if the serve is strong enough, to get to net and take the advantage.

Practice your serve—your opening move, your product launch routine—until it becomes second nature and your eyes can visualize the target as your muscles do their work.

When we wrote *The Purchasing Machine* in 2001, we surveyed 247 companies to evaluate their Best Practices, and we found that although none of them were high performers in all areas, there were some twenty Best Practices that built success, and our winners excelled at more than one of them. Honda, for instance, excels at supplier development but has been less concerned with computer systems. Others have the quality challenge knocked, but they have not advanced to address the decentralization/centralization optimization equation.

Looking back on our decisions that identified the twenty Best Practices in supply chain management and the Ten Best companies, we realized there is a twenty-first Best Practice, which has the most powerful message of all—*Spend Management*. We're talking about a method to capture billions of dollars of leveraged savings, real cash freed up that can be sent directly to the bottom line to enrich shareholder value; or, management can grow new products, new plants, new ideas, or reward employees, without robbing another company initiative.

Spend Management is the intelligent leveraging of all financial opportunities at high levels in the extended enterprise, and veteran supply managers are well acquainted with its potential. Spend Management is what IBM's Gene Richter used to save his company $9 billion. Richter's aggressive redirecting of procurement saved IBM and won his team the coveted Chairman's Award. It's a powerful combination of supreme commodity expertise, and competitive drive to be the absolute best in buying, worldwide.

Although it might be easier to focus solely on simple solutions such as kaizen and lean methods, these are only one segment of Best Practices that will create guaranteed returns for specific areas. It is difficult to extend lean practices to all areas of the enterprise because of the complexity of the task. Companies like Boeing have discovered that this is a monumental task, and many teams have been defeated by the never-ending challenge.

However, Spend Management works at the highest level of financial control from the moment a buyer starts to think. Any time a purchaser works with an engineering product idea, or when he pulls out his credit card and places an order, the best principles of Spend Management are activated. If this approach to money management can be used throughout the corporation, there is an opportunity to obtain a volume price. If the item has been sourced to dozens of different suppliers, there is an opportunity to consolidate; if engineers could be persuaded to design in a simpler, fewer-pieces part method there is a lifecycle cost-savings opportunity. If technology has changed, but the price has not, there will be savings available. And if suppliers can be persuaded to institute lean manufacturing Best Practices, they will find great savings in the elimination of waste. Spend Management finds the savings opportunities, weights the decisions, and points toward the best answer.

The probability of being killed in a lightning strike of a commercial airliner is nearly insignificant at one in four million. Yet, most of us are afraid to fly in a storm. The probability of dying from cancer or heart disease is higher, but many of us still smoke or have diets that destroy our health. *But when we say that Best Practices can help any company take 3 percent, 5 percent, 7 percent, or even 10 percent off its purchasing spend, we are not surprised when even the best demand a good road map, with pictures and a compass.*

We would like to think that the incredible billion-dollar payback potential of Spend Management—the twenty-first Best Practice—can be simply and powerfully adopted by virtually any enthusiastic company. But it won't. That's the reason we wrote this book. We know there is money out there, and we want to see procurement lead the corporation and realize the opportunity. We wish you luck in every one of your very profitable endeavors.

—Patricia E. Moody

Acknowledgments

So many supply chain leaders happily shared their expertise and experience. We thank them all—Marsha Begun; Jim Bergman; Jim Booth; Jim Cebula; Sophia Clemmer; Dave Curry, PLAN; Trung Dung; Lynne Hagerman; Dr. Robert Handfield; Doug Hathaway, Delphi Manager of Supplier Development; Beth Heinrich; Henri Irrthum, Vice President and Chief Procurement Officer, DuPont; H. Kamimura; Chris Lofgren; Michelle Malinowski; Jose Mejia, President of Lucent Supply Chain Networks; Dr. Robert Monczka; Chad Moody; Mark Preston, Respironics; Marilyn Rowe; John Sammut, President and CEO, Epic Technologies; Don Schneider; Nancy Q. Smith; and Tom Stuart.

THE
INCREDIBLE
PAYBACK

Introduction

The thrill is gone.

You are in the first seat of the intergalactic thrill ride of your life—you got on expecting a few twists and turns; the attendant locked you in the seat; and now your neck hurts, your hands grip the rail, pieces of clothing and popcorn boxes are flying by, and you've had enough, you want to get off. But the attendant won't hit the stop switch, and you and a few remaining ticket holders are hurled along at hundreds of miles per hour, until gravity slows the car to a full stop and you stagger off to solid ground.

When manufacturing and supply chain managers experience the losses and chaos of a big economic shift, their hearts stop, even when they knew the next big "adjustment" was coming. But it's the tectonic power of the Internet that has made the enormous shockwaves inescapably stronger and more immediate. Even managers in predictably cyclic industries, such as holiday toys, know that although good planning helps to soften the blows, bad news travels at nanosecond speed down an integrated supply chain. It is easier (and faster) to ramp up than to turn off the machines.

Cisco, for example, which is a model of planned outsourcing over global supply networks, shocked the market with a wash of red ink "adjustments." Other high-tech producers push inventory and capacity responsibilities back onto suppliers as they struggle for a foothold during big swings. Book publishers, automobile manufacturers, appliance producers, retail, and even some pharmaceuticals continue to wrestle for control as violent demand swings jerk them up and down. Second- and third-tier suppliers, the small- and medium-size companies whose growth rates have enriched our economy for years, have had the life squeezed out of them by their bigger customers. Life has gotten ugly out on the periphery of the supply chain, and we have no idea when the ride will stop.

Dave Nelson, vice president of global supply management at Delphi Corporation, and a forty-year veteran of the economic thrill ride, has experienced contrasting responses. "Most companies—100 percent of American ones—don't look at the long term," says Nelson. "When they do go into a downturn, it's like it's the first time they ever went into one—they haven't planned for it, and they react based on what they think the street will think."

Nelson sees different approaches from Toyota and Honda, where he worked for ten years, however. "I was at Honda during the 1991 recession. Honda had a 'no-layoff policy,' but the company sent a letter to everyone explaining the situation, and the grave need for people to take vacation—we called it 'no pay, no penalty.' Farmers, for instance, who wanted and needed to farm, were happy to have the summer off. With the traditional layoff formula, 1,260 people would have been targeted for cuts, but there were seven or eight hundred who went for the no pay/no penalty, leaving a few hundred." These associates were deployed to track quality issues; they placed phone calls to every customer who had ever bought a Honda—"millions of phone calls—and all of them added up to significant results," says Nelson, "when Honda won the J.D. Power Award."

Not only was the company able to retain valuable human assets, but the telephone campaign strengthened consumer relations. "Hundreds of surprised buyers took the trouble to write a note saying this was the first time anyone had ever called to see how they liked their Honda! So we survived a bad time with very positive results."

Why is a struggling economy and its deep swings so difficult to manage, and so severe and damaging to manufacturing and the supply chain? With ten years' talk about lean manufacturing and the Toyota Production System, aren't we finally in an era of instant manufacturing flexibility, responsiveness, and speed? And what happened to the power of giant ERP (Enterprise Requirements Planning) control systems? Is there anything managers on the ride can do to stop the pain and fear and *just get through it*?

Yes and no. Yes, the manager of a well-constructed supply chain can find ways to cut costs, other than squeezing suppliers and launching another round of layoffs. Companies like John Deere and Delphi have discovered simple methods to improve responsiveness and purchasing parts prices. But no, you won't find any of the survivors jumping off the ride until it's absolutely over and they have come to rest at the gate.

There is a basic imbalance right now between manufacturing and supply chain capabilities that managers need to understand in order to plan for market swings and to survive the current one. Producers can ramp up at Internet speed, but production is less responsive and infinitely less flexible to downturns; it's nearly impossible to slow down once the start button has been pushed. Web communications for procurement executives—buyers for companies like Flextronics, John Deere, Honda, and others—have provided purchasers with incredible global access and speed. For new product designs, mainline assemblers can put themselves into full production in a matter of months, and Internet auctions have further opened global price opportunities. In the steel business, for example, where companies like Deere continue to spend about 20 percent of their purchasing dollars, the World Wide Web and simple spreadsheet applications have allowed companies to save millions, without undertaking the more severe measures that a pure cost cutting focus would require.

We wrote *The Incredible Payback* because we think that the power of procurement to contribute to corporate financial health is understood by only a few visionary leaders—the potential is enormous, and barely touched. But the timing for spreading the good word could not be better.

Three critical supply chain strategies are proven high-payback approaches for survival in a roller-coaster economy:

1. Staff *up*.
2. Maintain high-level relationships.
3. Use simple systems to understand your own business costs and optimize wherever possible.

Staff Up

Whoa! During layoffs and shutdowns, is it really the time to staff *up*? Among the company leaders we named the Top Ten Supply Chain operations in our 2001 book *The Purchasing Machine, How the Top Ten Companies Use Best Practices to Manage Their Supply Chains* are American Express, GlaxoSmithKline, Harley-Davidson, Honda of America, IBM, Flextronics, Sun, and Deere. In these companies, supply management commands a leveraged key position in the enterprise. Purchasing staff are better prepared and compensated than the average purchasing geek; engineers rule, and managers understand the full value of their contribution to the corporate bottom line. And they are not afraid to talk about it.

Maintain High-Level Relationships

Close customer supplier communications, like the ones Delphi enjoys with other enterprise leaders, require high-level maintenance and trust around key issues—such as what products are on the launch pad, and where commodity risks prevail, or forecasts for key raw material prices. In the long term, these assets are difficult, if not impossible, to recapture.

Managing through a downturn requires that supply chain leaders identify those few critical commodities or value streams that must be closely watched; shift these items to high-level management monitoring, with daily operations handled by the best team members. Raw materials like steel, for instance, high volume items whose fluctuating price contribute a lion's share to many products cannot be left to manage themselves through traditional or routine distribution center channels.

For Big, Visible Payoffs, Use Simple Systems to Understand Your Own Business Costs and Optimize Wherever Possible

The payoff for massive manufacturing systems like ERP has, for many enterprises, never come. Companies like Buell Motorcycle and Auburn Industries, both suppliers with enormous product complexity and variety, have found alternative solutions however. They have innovated themselves into flexibility and responsiveness with smaller, off-the-shelf systems. Their stories are a fresh departure from two extremes of management thinking rampant in industry today: the lean thinkers who insist on pure process, unfettered by computer assists, and the ERP behemoths, who believe bigger (systems) are better. Each of these camps has found itself truly limited by a rigid approach to manufacturing management. Unable to see beyond their current obsessions, they find it difficult to build production capabilities that respond as quickly as the market demands.

For example, Dave Meyer, an engineer formerly working out of Deere's supplier development group, used Evolver, an off-the-shelf genetic algorithm package, combined with an Excel spreadsheet, to design in *less than one week* a simple but powerful scheduling method that determined best parts flow over a variety of machine tools, an exercise too complex for ordinary human minds, but one disregarded by traditional lean thinkers. Meyer knew that the endless combinations of parts and routings could be simplified with the power of the computer, and he knew that only a few combinations would truly meet all scheduling parameters for due dates and quality. *And he recognized that this was a problem that only a computer could solve.* The genetic algorithm approach to handling variety and complexity has been successfully implemented on a larger scale at GM, and at Deere's planter assembly line. Meyer made history for supply chain organizations who are stepping into the shoes of manufacturing planners. He found a better way, and he taught suppliers themselves how to harness this powerful but simple solution.

Managing through a downturn is still a painful and confusing experience, but there is a better way. In *The Incredible Payback*, we offer strong examples of smart management and systems strategies that will lighten the workload and even prepare an organization for better times ahead. Our recommendation to besieged managers is to look for The Incredible Payback—to employ the best of the best, continue to talk regularly with key customers and suppliers, and work for innovative solutions.

—Patricia E. Moody

Chapter 1

The Incredible Payback

How would your company like to spend 20 to 30 percent less *every day* on materials and services and still obtain even higher-quality finished products? Every day, companies lose billions of dollars in potential bottom-line profits because they are not doing strategic sourcing. Yet, it is much easier and faster for companies to deliver better profits through intelligent sourcing than it is for them to struggle to find and develop new markets or new products and plants, or new revenue streams.

Supply chain managers are currently in the best position they have ever been, capable of making significant contributions to enterprise profitability and growth because they control 50 to 90 percent of product costs. Outsourced materials and services have risen to the point of 85 to 90 percent in many industries, including automotive, where suppliers contribute most of the parts, systems, and design help to final assembly plants. In the best supply management organizations—for example, companies such as Honda—the supply managers' power and span of responsibility is growing. The top purchasing departments are designed to do more than buy or move material; the functions of manufacturing, distribution, and logistics all report into the head of strategic supply management, as well as planning and buying of big spends. And the best procurement groups have discovered that by combining functions—from inbound material, through processing, and out to logistics—they can make an even bigger contribution to high-impact profit generation.

If companies want to realize the full potential of supply management in their drive for better profits, they need to look carefully at the capabilities of supply management as the strong and significant contributor to a company's income statement. They need to recognize the power of an increased purchasing spend and put the responsibility where it belongs, in the hands of supply management professionals.

Unfortunately, even in difficult and changeable economic times, too few companies have discovered and begun mining the full power of high-performance strategic sourcing. For many operations, Spend Management is an intriguing phrase that is not connected with the way they buy. However, the leading supply chains in companies such as Honda of America, John Deere, IBM, Motorola, and Delphi Corporation are organized and staffed to create and execute high-level strategic visions that generate significant profits—paybacks that reach multiples of original investments in procurement people and systems. In these high performers, procurement goals are aligned with corporate objectives, and profitability is key. The winners and their enterprise partners, producers who emphasize the power of strategic sourcing and purchasing, are organized to take a longer-term view. To capture lost profits, they have transformed the way manufacturers buy; they know that every dollar spent in people, systems, and especially materials, must show big paybacks. And they are looking to create an ongoing stream of increased savings.

More, More, More . . .

When companies discover the power of strong financial returns—that is, the power of procurement to send more profits to their shareholders, to hit the market with more new products than the competition, and to hire new talent for growth—*they want more*. Spend Management and strategic sourcing leverage enable companies like United Technologies and Delphi Corporation as well as smaller ones to cut through tactical issues and raise performance to higher-than-ever levels.

The Domino Effect

Big numbers attract big commitment, and inevitably, strategic sourcing execs report that their substantial gains capture management's attention. And with the positive momentum generated when The Incredible Payback is put into play comes greater success, more responsibility, better rewards, and even greater challenges for supply management professionals. As Honda and Delphi understand, the power of procurement executives who can visualize, propose, and deliver The Incredible Payback is irreplaceable. The Incredible Payback is vital to long-term growth and profitability.

Just What Is The Incredible Payback?

Every day we make dozens of little decisions, and occasionally big ones, that we hope will pay back big. A hundred-thousand-dollar college degree, for example, over a lifetime of work, should pay off more than ten times its original investment. Smart real estate investments in San Francisco and Boston have paid off over tenfold in twenty years. One-dollar lottery tickets paid off twice for a Massachusetts contractor who purchased both winning scratch tickets four months apart at the same variety store; the first $1 investment yielded $25,000 in pre-tax earnings, but the second came in at $10 million—"enough," said the laconic carpenter and winter plowman, "to give up snow plowin'"!

Or, consider the expected payback made when a homeowner installs a new heating system. With a $5,000 initial investment, the projected monthly savings of $50 to $100 are significant and real, but it will take the homeowner five to ten years to reach the breakeven point. How much quicker that payback would be if he were not only using fifty dollars less fuel per month but the price of home heating oil dropped to a half a cent per gallon! Now that would be an Incredible Payback!

Some decisions, like lottery tickets, carry higher risk than others. A good market analysis of San Francisco real estate trends in the post–World War II boom years would have shown a strong upward trend with not too much risk. The trick to bet making, of course, is to find or create investments whose risk is predictably minimal or nonexistent. And where shareholders want to see a steady stream of nice dividend and stock price appreciation, corporate executives may choose to minimize risk and take the surer, safer route to profits.

Manufacturers and retail operations look at investment payback in similar ways. Requests for new equipment, new people and plants, even new materials, undergo sharp scrutiny when they require borrowing to meet payments or spending from projected cash flows. Every dollar spent represents a hoped-for return in profits and growth; even once-sacred categories of capital equipment and materials come under the lens of budget-conscious managers with an eye toward doing better with what they have. Downward market shifts, technology change, and consumers' taste for better, bigger, and faster guarantee that the game stays exciting and unpredictable.

How many new CNC machines or robotic welders, or even Enterprise Resource Planning (ERP) systems, have companies bought, for example, and based their breakeven projections on huge start-up volumes, full-speed ahead runs that never appeared? On paper the purchase justification for that multimillion-dollar machine looked unbeatable, but then, when management watched a kaizen project replace the behemoth with a single work cell of seven smaller machines, the numbers told a different story.

Supply Chain Executives Manage Risk

Supply chain professionals are critical power players in the financial risk/reward games all companies play. They manage the numbers that make the difference in corporate profits; they control big spends; and they have the power to put that spend where they will make an immediate impact on future growth. They can grow a capable and loyal supply base, or they can accumulate hundreds of average performers. They can make new product launches successful and profitable events, or they can cause delays and create unhappy customers. They can reward good suppliers and develop partnerships that grow everyone's profits, or they can misuse their power to leverage short-term price and contract advantages that drive good suppliers away.

Smart supply chain executives can make other departments shine; they can make design engineers happy and take the headaches out of production schedules. The spend they manage touches just about every company's functions, from engineering and even marketing down through production and distribution. Given manufacturing flexibility and instantaneous communications, they can deliver on creative and powerful ways to beat the game and win.

The power of a high-performing supply chain team combined with excellent suppliers and a brilliant central control system is what separates average performers from superior ones. Excellent supply chain management can meet all the basic market demands of flexibility and quality, *plus* it will raise the bar on price performance four or five notches by achieving billion-dollar cost savings that hit the bottom line again and again.

With such great and rich potential sitting at desks and cubicles scattered around headquarters and division plants, why aren't more companies seizing the billion-dollar opportunities lying in supply chain management? Would the transformations achieved with huge savings not carry company dreams farther than they ever hoped? If every supply management group and each purchasing buyer or planner knew how to achieve The Incredible Payback, why would companies struggle with insignificant projects and ineffectual methods?

Big Plans, Big Numbers, Big Results

The answer, of course, is that far too many good companies—even those operations skilled in people management and teams, cost accounting, and all the other discrete challenges of making a company work and grow—are operating procurement at a kindergarten level. These companies do not see the potential for substantial gains; and they have few examples to lead them toward an Incredible Payback. They use supply management as a material flow device, a disintegrated, loosely organized pipeline or network in which production opens valves that spill out necessary materials. If they could see that same network, however, as an enormously complex cash transaction system with currency flowing in and out of dozens of ATMs, they might be able to tally up the grand total of the spend as well as the possible savings (see Figure 1–1).

Spend Management demands, however, that companies look at their networks of rapidly moving materials, and slower moving inventories, as real money, cash. Visualize the network of some five hundred suppliers required to produce a single automobile constructed with five or six thousand pieces. Every dollar spent to

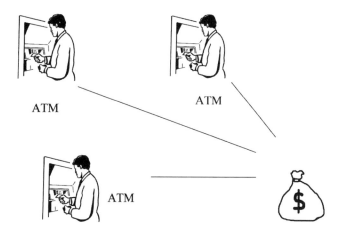

Figure 1-1. Paths to The Incredible Payback.

mine aluminum, ship it to the foundry, run the furnaces, cast the engine block, trim the raw castings and polish them to a jeweler's finish, and then test the results, is a dollar that flowed through numerous pipeline nodes. Tracking the cash flows for an aluminum engine would be a challenge, especially if we wanted to repeat the process with five thousand other automotive components in order to construct a series of snapshots capturing all the components' cash flows in and out of various operations.

But what if we concentrated on the $2,000 per unit cost multiplied by one thousand units per month that it took to build $2 million worth of cars, and managed it so well that we made it work? Stated simply, one year's production runs would total a spend of $24 million, and even a 1 percent change in that spend would have an immediate impact. A 1 percent increase can throw the retail price out of the market, but a 1 percent cost reduction would immediately free up about one quarter of a million dollars. That kind of aggregate potential is the focus of Spend Management, not the endless focus on too many details. When the big number, the $24 million, comes into focus for the first time, it clarifies what should be done tactically with the thousands of smaller numbers.

The Incredible Payback is a way to see big numbers, a magnification lens that allows companies to think big and aim for significant returns. No company wants to turn itself inside out to produce decimal point returns over a twelve-month period, yet that is what happens on a daily basis in traditional operations that work with disappointing incremental gains.

Investors and shareholders want returns that at least match the inflation rate; beyond that, companies need cash to *grow* in order to fuel new products, new technologies, new plants, new hires, and more training, as well as capital equipment and ordinary operating expenses.

The Incredible Payback Opportunity Areas

Every company that buys materials such as plastic resin, chips, packaging, and services (including travel, employee benefits, training, and other nonphysical but important items) has the opportunity to find The Incredible Payback because being in business means moving cash—taking it in, counting it, and spending it—for material, labor, and services to create profit. In the computer industry, for instance, material purchases include raw materials, components, assemblies, and even complete units, ready to be labeled and shipped off to retailers and consumers. For outsourced electronics, the cash movement in and out of the network nodes is incredibly complex to follow, while in the automotive industry, where design-to-ship times stretch out to a year or more, dozens of opportunities lie waiting for managers to find The Incredible Payback. Every purchase and every transaction is an opportunity, and in total, all these cash transactions tally up to The Incredible Payback. The trick is to find the tools that allow managers to focus in on the best opportunities and the richest payback areas.

It's Not Just a Hammer

In the 1980s and 1990s, many companies looked for savings opportunities by focusing on a single powerful cost-reduction tool. Reengineering, for example, took layers of "excess" organization structure and communications links out of operations; self-managed work teams displaced foremen, supervisors, and managers. Huge ERP computer systems, which replaced manual transactions and tied dozens of disparate functions together to make every task visible and measurable, were expected to generate big savings. Each of these single-minded approaches, however, had short-lived results that damaged other critical functions.

Our approach to achieving The Incredible Payback is equally focused and single-minded; the methods are also relatively simple and straightforward. However, there is more than one path to great paybacks. When companies are strong in supplier relationships and supplier development, they will achieve huge gains very quickly. In fact, that is what many companies have tackled; for more than ten years, many manufacturers and their suppliers have applied kaizen and other lean methods to production with encouraging results. Unfortunately, although these gains can be sustained at good levels year after year, they frequently stall out and require a big effort to restart the process. However, there are many other ways to achieve significant savings. We know that companies at the very beginning of their journey can easily achieve 1 or 2 percent reductions in their spend without even a headache. For million-dollar supply chains, those savings translate to millions of dollars of profits for new plants, new people, training, equipment, or just plain shareholders' returns.

Let's look at a simple example of how powerful an impact supply chain focus on Spend Management can have on a company's income statement.

Allied Auto is an established automotive supplier with some

very demanding customers. The car industry is restructuring and growing in new global opportunity areas, but consumers expect better prices and performance all around. Naturally, Allied's big customers transfer the pressure right on to their supplier.

Allied's CEO is not happy with corporate profitability, but he is not eager to undertake the measures so many other companies have taken—layoffs and plant closings. Sales are predicted to be strong and spread over a diverse product portfolio, but the board is impatient with Allied's profit picture. They want margins and better yields, and they want to see the money flow immediately!

Allied's current income statement shows 88 percent of its revenues spent on purchased materials and services, and manufacturing, with the balance going to engineering, research and development (R&D), and salary, general and administrative (SG&A), thereby leaving nothing for profits.

Revenue from sales	$2.5 billion
Cost of goods sold:	
Cost of purchased goods and services (55% of sales)	1.375B
Manufacturing in-house (33%)	.825
Engineering and R & D (6%)	.15
SG & A (Selling, General and Administrative) (6%)	.15
Profit	$0
Five year plan for 10% savings = $.25B, or $50M/year.	

CEO Richard Daniels would like to see a solid 10 percent margin, or $.25 billion, over five years, which would release millions of dollars annually to the coffers.

Allied's choices are numerous. The board could simply edict a 10-percent-across-the-board price increase and wait to hear the fireworks from Allied's bigger, and more powerful, customers. The next—and more likely—possibility, one that no one is eager to contemplate, would be to take plant capacity and personnel down by 10 percent. The board knows, however, that taking millions of dollars in savings and restructuring charges would not inspire market confidence in the company's future, nor would it allow Allied to retain the heart and soul of its future, its cadres of engineers and technologists. Plant closings would also cascade down and decimate the supply chain, a hit that would work to the benefit of competitors.

But wait, might there be another savings route, one that would have collateral benefits as well? That is where The Incredible Payback comes in!

Any good purchasing operation can deliver 1 or 2 percentage points in savings simply by paying more attention to purchases and suppliers. This is the beginner's level, and Allied could easily capture a few million dollars without adding personnel or restructuring the supply chain. But Daniels and his impatient stockholders want more, without a price increase.

By far the biggest segment of product costs lies in the $1.375 billion line item for the purchasing spend. A 10 percent savings here, the CEO's $50 million annual target would represent only 3.6 percent of the total annual spend. But how realistic is it for Allied to try for it?

Savings Levels—First, Beginners

The average, traditional purchasing operation can, without too much difficulty, cut its spend by 1 to 2 percent just by paying closer attention to how it buys. This is the beginner's level, and it does not require big organizational changes or significant investment to earn 1 percent savings. Operations can easily achieve 1 to 2 percent payback by simply instituting suggestion systems or by doing some preliminary supply base consolidation.

Intermediate- and Expert-Level Savings

Companies that use some of our Best Practices can achieve 3 to 5 percent year to year with steady attention to the basics and continuous improvement. Surpassing 5 percent savings every year is a challenge best suited for expert supply chain groups with high-performance suppliers, excellent communications, and very responsive operations—that is, the best of the best.

The first year is always the easiest as sharp eyes spot low-hanging fruit throughout the supply base. In general, years two and three open up opportunities for deeper savings with strategic sourcing and supplier development. Taking spend reduction performance to the levels that companies such as Honda and Toyota consistently reach is the big challenge, one that requires the best people and tools throughout the supply chain.

Exponential Savings

Most companies start a "lean journey" without first addressing Spend Management's bigger opportunities. They may do lean projects first because they are visible and approachable, or because they have seen fabulous results from Toyota or Honda. Perhaps they don't think of starting Spend Management because they do not have a centralized procurement structure that facilitates high-yield Spend Management.

Manufacturing and purchasing occupy such politically separate and different worlds in most organizations—reporting into different managers—that many operations tend to stick to very visible process work in manufacturing: Lean implementations and Spend Management appear to occupy different areas of the supply chain. Good supplier development and internal kaizen methods are powerful, but they are not enough, however, nor do they address the bigger payback potential at the shop floor level, so they cannot address the total spend.

Furthermore, it is difficult to sustain the gains from good kaizen, and the challenge of taking lean methods to all operations internally, as well as to all suppliers, is overwhelming for many operations.

Kaizen Payback

Payback for BP, Honda's kaizen methodology, has been continuous and impressive, as it grew expertise inside the company and outside in the supply base. In less than twenty years, Honda built a self-reliant automobile/motorcycle complex in central Ohio. What started as a knockdown assembly plant largely dependent for direction and materials on headquarters in Japan, quickly grew to include many high-performing suppliers located within twenty-four hours of the assembly lines.

Some suppliers were brand-new start-ups, that is, greenfield sites open to building product "the Honda Way." Others were joint ventures between Japanese and U.S. companies that were already familiar with Honda's lean method, called BP (for Best Position, Best Productivity, Best Product, Best Price, and Best Partners). But for many suppliers, this well-sought-after business was a challenge. They needed help, such as extra hands in the form of Honda purchasing engineers, to smooth out glitches and remove waste. The objective for both partners—customer and supplier—was to produce perfect product and make a healthy profit, and so it made sense that Honda and its suppliers would take advantage of Honda BP to enable the best production possible.

Honda BP

In total, Honda BP, launched in 1976 in Japan and in 1990 in North America, had touched almost 100 companies and over 120 projects after eight years at the transplant. More than 120,000 supplier associates were affected by the BP approach. Best of all, the BP report card showed the following paybacks:[1]

Productivity gains overall	47%
(total pieces per man per hour before BP compared	
to pieces per man per hour after BP)	
Quality improvement overall	30%
Cost-down overall	**7.25%**

Furthermore BP, as well as other Honda improvement techniques such as Value Analysis and Value Engineering, helped to reduce the actual cost of purchased parts for the 1998 Accord by more than 20 percent. These savings were generated not from cost avoidance but from actual savings in material and labor on purchased parts.

In Japanese, the word *kaizen* means "to make better" (see Figure 1–2). By the late 1990s, many other progressive innovators had heard about Honda and started their own kaizen projects with amazing, even better than expected, results. For most early adopters, kaizen was a survival strategy that came along just in time to free up buckets of cash and save customers. Kaizen saved Lantech, a Louisville, Kentucky, packaging equipment producer, a pioneer in lean or kaizen methods. Lantech used kaizen to redesign products and power new product introductions, as well as to take waste out of shop floor production and material flows.

In general, companies can expect to see efficiency improvements rise from 20 to 50 percent; inventory reductions (raw material, in process, and components) are drastic and immediate, from 20 to 80 percent; distance traveled on the production floor, another way of looking at inventory cost and inefficiency, is usually cut in half, with some areas showing reductions up to 90 percent; productivity, a measure of how well production uses labor, equipment, and materials—as in number of pieces produced per hour—improves by 10 to 50 percent.

For many companies, Best Practices means continuous improvement, and when companies want to work hard on continu-

Figure 1-2. Japanese character for kaizen.

ous improvement, they start with kaizen. Whether the projects are called Honda BP, Kaizen Blitzes, lean manufacturing, or simply the Toyota Production System, they use many of the same simple tools to rethink the way manufacturing works, usually starting with a good pilot project that captures low-hanging fruit to build enthusiasm and process understanding. Investment is minimal; and in fact, many kaizen projects remove costly capital equipment as well as inventory.

The Kaizen Blitz

Honda's BP process was designed as a thirteen-week experience, from training and data gathering through implementation. Other methods, however, were developed to see rapid payback in as little as four or five days. One of these techniques, dubbed The Kaizen Blitz by the Association for Manufacturing Excellence, introduced thousands of employees to Japanese methods. Kaizen Blitz's claims were enticing: "When was the last time your company improved productivity from 20 percent to 60 percent in only four days? Or cut inventory by 50 percent in the same amount of time?" These remarkable results were delivered by teams of employees guided by facilitators. Employees learned how to work as a team to tackle problems from the shop floor and, more important, how to solve them quickly. The Kaizen Blitz teaches a highly focused process aimed at producing incremental performance improvements in narrowly targeted areas. It is a powerful technique that delivers rapid, breakthrough improvements at lighting speed. A Blitz involves everyone across an organization—managers and workers alike. It is a low-cost, hands-on process in which all team members are equal and everyone gets his hands dirty.

Paybacks are significant, with a range of performance data depending on the level of expertise of team members and degree of difficulty of the project. However, Kaizen Blitz experts generally track big paybacks in the following areas:[2]

Kaizen Blitz Paybacks:

Set-up time reduction	70–90%
Productivity improvement	20–60%
Process time reduction	40–80%
Inventory reduction	30–70%
Walking distance reduction	40–90%

These results were compiled from more than fifty Kaizen Blitz companies, including Critikon (a Johnson and Johnson Company), Hamilton Standard, Jacobs Manufacturing, Pratt & Whitney, Wiremold, Microtouch, Nypro, Boston Scientific, US Robotics, and Rockwell Automation.

Sustaining the Gains

Not all results have been perfect, however, because many companies stall out after initial gains. Blitz projects tend to have great initial impact; companies plateau, however, when they attempt to apply the new methodology to all work areas. They have difficulty sustaining the gains, and they may rest at improved, but not excellent, performance. Nearly every company that has begun its lean journey reports great learning experiences, solid productivity gains, and, initially, freed-up cash. The challenge is to maintain that same rate of progress. Delphi Corporation, however, a frequent winner of the Shingo Prize and a leader in lean manufacturing—one of the components of The Incredible Payback—continues to report huge and significant gains in production as well as in its supply base.

The Challenge of Migrating Lean to the Whole Supply Base

Although most operations start with simple lean pilot projects conducted on one line or one internal production area, it is more difficult to take internal lean methods quickly or easily "outside" to the supply base. Small- and medium-size suppliers may not have the resources in-house to work on kaizen, and they may need help with the lean development assists. Plus, their processes must be well understood before they can be changed. Not all customers can offer their suppliers the kind of skilled lean development resources that these projects require.

But, when organizations combine strong Spend Management and strategic sourcing with high-yield lean or kaizen processing performance from excellent suppliers, they realize the full power of The Incredible Payback. If management and control of the corporate spend is in place, but supplier processes are unpredictable and costly, companies can achieve The Incredible Payback by addressing their weaknesses in the supply base first. Either way, by first managing and controlling the strategic spend a new way, then improving the supply base, the results are significant.

We will talk more about proven results and how to plan and measure gains as we look at success stories. But let's be clear about the potential for gains. If you follow the example of our leading purchasing operations, your company can expect significant payback to appear quickly—in less than a year. When gains are easy to achieve and quite significant, as your organization's skill levels rise, cumulative gains continue and the game will become more challenging.

Benchmarking the Possibilities

In the late 1990s, three consulting firms—McKinsey, Arthur D. Little, and AT Kearney—benchmarked a group of companies, trying to identify what supply chain practices differentiated them from other firms, and what practices were best and worst.

McKinsey looked at six best practice groupings—strategy, organization, execution, specifications and make buy, supplier management, and logistics and inventory management. AT Kearney ranked the best of the best in manufacturing, resource conversion (companies like Boise Cascade and Chevron), and services. One of the benchmarked companies was Honda of America.

Honda: Best Practices Results and Data

Key supply management metrics showed significant differences among companies as well. In the critical area of quality performance, or parts per million (ppm), Honda showed quality levels well above other leading U.S. competitors' scores of 300 ppm. Delivery performance, a critical measure of on-time delivery capability, is vital in the automotive industry, where shutting a line down for even one minute has been estimated to cost about $26,000. Honda's delivery performance ranked at 99.9 percent—nearly 100 percent of all parts (components and systems) arrived at the assembly plant on time, complete—not early and not late—to the line's requirement date. The third measure of supply chain performance, inventory, stood at less than twenty-five days among the leaders. But again, Honda showed far superior control, running with less than four days total inventory in 1997. Two more measures of superior supply management, the amount of material sourced to preferred suppliers (100 percent at Honda and 85 percent among other leaders) and training hours per person (greater than eighty at Honda) showed the gap between procurement Best Practices at this transplant and its sourcing competitors.

Furthermore, the measure of procurement's ability to manage a spend well, to keep costs within the inflation rate, or to beat industry average increases, showed great disparity between the best and the worst performers. The best performers were able to develop a five-year savings plan and execute it. Clearly, companies like Honda and its suppliers were doing something vastly different with purchasing.

Deere and Company's Experience with Best Practices and Spend Management

In the late 1990s, John Deere, the global agriculture and heavy equipment manufacturer, was doing quite well for itself. With sales of $13 billion and worldwide employment of more than 45,000 people, the company was able to weather periodic sector downturns and continue to show nice profits.

Deere could have done better, however, because the supply management operation was not structured to yield The Incredible Payback. Highly decentralized, with more than 14,000 active suppliers worldwide, it was hard, if not impossible, for the company to get a handle on its spend—what the company was buying in raw materials and production components and where—the first step toward understanding The Incredible Payback. No single system summarized exactly what the company was buying in raw materials and production components, and from whom, and how often.

Individually, Deere's decentralized plants could point to very successful operations, but centrally, it was impossible for Deere to leverage its global size and optimize supply chain power. Manufacturing's global operations numbered seventy-two, each of which maintained a separate supply chain, with different prices and specifications.

And the redundancies appeared in global product distribution as well. For example, bearings that were used in production in Sweden, Japan, and South Korea were each sourced locally to a different supplier. Steel, another heavy hitter and a common denominator in many of Deere's globally produced products, was controlled and bought by a highly decentralized group of supply chains. And yet, with a $13 billion spend, even a savings of 1 percent per year would have returned $130 million to corporate coffers, more than enough to fund a run of new products or a couple new plants.

But like many big and successful corporations, the problem was not worrisome, and there was little incentive to struggle with major change. Best Practices dictate, however, that to improve returns, big changes in supply management are the proven way to go.

The Two Proven Paths to The Incredible Payback

There are two approaches to achieving bigger profits driven by supply chain returns. These two comprehensive approaches, combined, produce The Incredible Payback:

1. Best Practices—twenty maturity index points that define high-level supply chain operations practices
2. Spend Management—strategic sourcing that manages and controls the spend

Payback for Best Practices and Spend Management

Let's look at the expected payback, or yields, for these two different approaches. Since most operations started to upgrade some of their supplier relationship and procurement programs well before Spend Management, we'll start with paybacks for Best Practices first.

Best Practice Paybacks

We took a look back at procurement leaders as we rounded the fifteen-year mark in quality and delivery systems, and the performance gap was striking. We know that if companies address purchasing Best Practices the way the high performers have, they will experience the same remarkable paybacks that early adopters of just-in-time (JIT), lean principles, the Toyota Production System, and Six Sigma quality have experienced.[3]

Metrics	Leaders' performance	1993	1996
Quality (ppm)	under 300 ppm	5426	2339
Delivery performance	Over 95%	76%	85%
Total Inventory in Days	Under 25	40	31
% Sourced Preferred	Over 85%	75%	80%
Training hours/person	Over 80	46	32

With a Six Sigma goal of 99.9996 percent perfection (only 3.4 defects per million), our data showed that there is always opportunity to improve. Delivery performance—the number of days before or after the promise date when the material is actually received—truly reflects how well the supply chain is meeting market demand. Clearly, the difference between over 95 percent on time performance and 76 percent reflects the enormous cost of missing schedule—payroll for dozens of expeditors, overtime, and premium shipments, all unnecessary expenses eliminated by Best Practices. How profitable can a facility be when a quarter of scheduled incoming material is not there, or when more than a month of twelve months' potential profits sits untouched and rusting in inventory?

Best Practices in quality, inventory, and delivery clearly cost less than bad performance!

Most companies are familiar with a few of the twenty Best Practices applied to raise the manufacturing performance of producers and suppliers in critical quality, performance, and cost areas. In manufacturing and in white collar areas like order administration, engineering and quality, quality methods, JIT, the Toyota Production System, and other lean manufacturing methods have enabled many producers to streamline processes and eliminate waste, as they increase productivity, cut lead times, and improve quality. These efforts usually fall under Best Practice #2, Supplier Development, because purchasing, which is concerned with quality and delivery problems with purchased material, will take a hard look at supplier processes first. With each new method, producers have been able to improve quality as they lay out new production flows, train workers, and redesign work to improve productivity and reduce waste.

The Twenty Best Practices That Define High-Level Supply Chain Operations Practices[4]

Best Practice #1: Cost Management—Cost management includes target pricing, cost tables, jikon (Japanese-style customer/supplier meeting), and kaizen productivity improvement techniques.

Best Practice #2: Supplier Development—Included in supplier development are quality teams and supplier engineering. Honda, the leader in supplier development, measures the effectiveness of supplier development by percent of localization, ppm (parts per million) quality, on-time delivery, supplier involvement in new product and other technical issues, and training time.

Best Practice #3: Value Analysis (Value Engineering)—The careful analysis of design early in the new product cycle to determine best materials, best tooling, and best manufacturing processes.

Best Practice #4: Nontraditional Purchasing—Maintenance Repair Operations (MRO), indirect materials and services, and other nontraditional purchased items.

Best Practice #5: Supplier Quality Circles—When Honda started to produce vehicles in North America, its first approach to helping suppliers raise their quality levels was to create dozens of supplier quality circles for training, general discussions, and problem solving.

Best Practice #6: Training—Internal training for purchasing professionals includes benchmarking and formal training in supplier development, quality, project management, etc. Externally, training for suppliers may cover the same areas as well as specific technology issues.

Best Practice #7: Supplier Information Sharing—This includes study groups, seminars, and management meetings.

Best Practice #8: Supplier Conference—Honda, Harley-Davidson, and other Best Practice leaders sponsor annual supplier conferences in which suppliers are recognized for their quality and delivery performance as well as for technology leadership.

Best Practice #9: Supplier Performance Reporting—The best organizations consolidate supplier performance reporting into a single "report card" that contains all key metrics.

Best Practice #10: Supplier Surveys—Every customer wants to retain the best suppliers, and one way to determine if the relationship is working well is to ask suppliers to evaluate the customer's processes. Supplier surveys that are conducted by a third party uncover a gold mine of partnership issues and point to productive solutions. For examples of supplier surveys used by Honda and Motorola, see *Breakthrough Partnering: Creating a Collective Enterprise Advantage.*[5]

Best Practice #11: Delivery Improvement—A delivery improvement program is a focused, continuous program to work with suppliers who make the highest negative impact on the customer's delivery schedules.

Best Practice #12: Tool and Technical Assistance Centers—Best Practice leaders maintain tooling and technical support centers solely to assist suppliers with expertise that they might not have in all component areas. The inclusion of these technical assists in purchasing or purchasing engineering emphasizes their strategic value.

Best Practice #13: Supplier Support (SWAT) Team—Supplier support (SWAT) teams are groups of dedicated experts who assist suppliers in various ways by arranging meetings, study groups, and seminars; or, they may be rapid response teams that can respond to supply emergencies.

Best Practice #14: Loaned Executives—When a supplier loses a key manager or technical employee, finding and locating a replacement can take up to a year, an unacceptable time for JIT schedules. At one point, Honda has had as many as fifteen professionals loaned out at one time to suppliers.

Best Practice #15: Early Supplier Involvement—Chrysler's breakthrough platform teams, colocating purchasing and design pros, and better product development software allow the most competitive enterprises to involve suppliers from concept through final design.

Best Practice #16: New Model Development Group—Some excellent producers invest in a dedicated team in purchasing to working with engineers and designers on product launch.

Best Practice #17: Written Strategy for Every Supplier, Every Part/Commodity—One of the most important tasks in Spend Management is to develop a written strategy for every supplier, and every part or commodity. This document addresses performance history, technology trends, as well as price and specification data.

Best Practice #18: Strategic Planning and Administration— Supply chain's strategic role includes planning for new plant and new sources to meet increased capacity requirements, as well as developing contingency and other strategic plans for emergencies and market drops. If purchasing does not participate at this level of corporate strategy, profit plans are unrealistic.

Best Practice #19: Career Path Planning and Academic Outreach Programs—In the past fifteen years, group opportunities to manage and develop high-performing supply management processionals have exploded. Resources from organization such as Michigan State, San Diego University, Arizona State, the Institute of Supply Management (ISM), and specialized consulting groups continue to enrich their course offerings. The best programs are used by customers, suppliers, and competitors alike.

Best Practice #20: Purchasing Systems—Systems that manage spend and control buying and material movement should ideally be linked to suppliers and internal users. However, smaller innovative software solutions may offer great flexibility and value. The best supply chain performers often use a mix of big data accumulators and smaller, agile problem solvers and analysis solutions.

Starting Out on the Right Foot to Build Best Practices

Even Honda and Toyota, the best of the best automotive operations that have pioneered clean process and a unique approach to procurement, are continually challenged by market competition. They know that their capabilities must be ready to move with continuous change. The performance gap, the huge chasm between performance that meets market demands and limited progress toward the ideal, requires consistently superior performance.

The first four Best Practices plus #16 New Model Development Group and #18 Strategic Planning and Administration were key to Honda's early work on taking costs and waste out of the supply chain. Although most operations start with only one or two of the five, it is possible to make simultaneous progress working with the following five initiatives.

1. Cost Management
2. Supplier Development
3. Value Engineering or Value Analysis
4. Indirect, MRO and Nontraditional materials and services procurement
5. Supplier Quality Circles

Incredible Payback Gains

Figure 1–3 illustrates the bottom-line potential of three approaches to cost management:

1. Keeping up with the purchased priced index (tracks inflation)
2. Adopting some Best Practices, without a sharp, focused Strategic Sourcing approach that targets Spend Management
3. A cost focus that draws on all opportunities offered by Best Practices, including Spend Management's consolidated buy and leveraged spend

Organizations that gear performance to follow the purchased price index are planning for average performance—nothing exceptional, no surprises, no big competitive wins. This type of "getting by" strategy guarantees that procurement will not take center

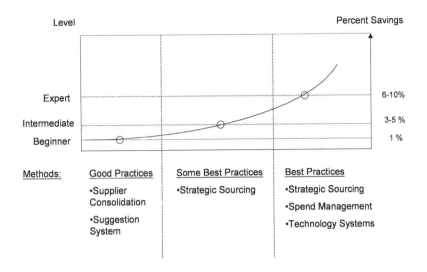

Figure 1–3. Supply management savings levels.

stage in any cost-cutting drive; similarly, it is clear that when top management is looking for significant profit growth, they will not turn to supply management whose work is at this "gentlemen's C" level.

Honda and Toyota transplant centers, however, show that their focused cost approach (#3) consistently yields savings of one-quarter of their total spend. Think about it—if your company routinely buys $1 million per year in materials and services, production and nonproduction (the spend), Best Practices will save 25 percent of that, or $250,000. If your company spend totals $1 billion per year, Best Practices will net more than $250 million a year. It's hard to ignore the potential when the proof continues to grow.

Making an Investment in Best Practices

Leveling up supply base performance through adoption of Best Practices and operating at a more mature and dedicated professional level does not come without some up-front costs. At

Honda's Marysville, Ohio, complex, the purchasing function encompasses more than four hundred professionals. Yet, for Honda, staffing up to develop and support a strong, local supply base was not a question of "How much?" but "When?" Training, job rotations, new systems, all the resources that add power and variety to a supply management group's potential, are expense items that should pay their way many times over.

John Deere added 175 new strategic supply management positions: 100 for supplier development, 50 cost management specialists, and 25 Best Practice specialists. Delphi Corporation added cost-and-systems and supplier development experts. And at Respironics, a high-growth medical equipment producer at the beginning of Incredible Payback work, two new supply management positions at headquarters, and training for upcoming kaizen projects, plus twenty days of consulting, were required to launch the campaign.

The Second Path to The Incredible Payback—Spend Management

Spend Management is a new term that describes the management of all expenditures for purchased materials and services, from metal and plastic components to temporary help and travel expenses, all the checks that companies pay out to stay in business. In most operations, companies have only a partial picture of what it really costs—how much they spend in total—to make their product. They typically skip advertising expenses or some personnel benefits, but even office supplies and production repair materials should be included in the total spend. Yet, all these categories of expenditures are part of a corporation's total spend, and the best purchasing executives understand that every dollar counts. If your company does not know how much it spends on specific commodities or services, or with specific suppliers, it will be difficult to leverage the power of a large spend to achieve a good payback.

When purchasing functions are decentralized, however, it may be impossible to pull all the spend data together in a single document. That is what must be done eventually, but in a decentralized operation, it may be necessary to pick a different starting point. A good place to begin is to gather at minimum the material, labor, and indirect materials required by production to make products. This information is usually available from the cost accounting system, and it should be fairly reliable.

We emphasize the importance of gathering all relevant cost data whenever it is possible, because it is important to establish a baseline against which managers can plan and monitor Spend Management.

Spend Management at John Deere and Company

In 1998 John Deere took a hard look at its purchasing results in comparison with recognized Best Practice leaders and industry average performance. Although the typical North American off-road equipment producer maintained year-to-year purchased parts price increases that were well below the purchased price index—a tracking number that grows about 2 percent per year—there was an enormous and growing gap between acceptable results and the purchased costs of Japanese transplant high performers. The Japanese transplants' total spend or purchased costs continued a steady drop to well below other producers' prices. Traditional purchasing practices could not explain the simultaneous drop in purchased costs linked to higher quality and features found in transplant products. What would allow the transplants to continue to show such incredible cost differences?

The company spend totaled approximately 7.1 billion per year (70 percent of global manufacturing costs) by maintaining what it felt was an acceptable 2.6 percent yearly increase between 1992 and 1998—well below the typical purchased price index. Supply chain managers realized they absorbed an additional $560 million in costs per year, or more than one-half billion dollars in additional spend! These millions of dollars of cost increases scattered through the company's purchase of production and nonproduction items, such as travel and benefits, were unexamined increases. No one really knew if they were necessary, or if they were contracted for or agreed upon, or how the suppliers were billing—truly, these cost increases "just seemed to happen!"

Furthermore, despite high growth, and market and currency swings, new plants and new products, the Japanese transplants still showed total spend that dropped predictably and consistently from 3 to 5 percent per year. Clearly, the transplants' procurement operations were doing something radically different, but North American producers, who were inclined to accept "normal" cost increases, were oblivious.

The 3 Percent Factor

Deere managers asked themselves: What would happen to our growing $7 billion spend if we targeted savings by simply leveling off cost increases and maintained a nearly flat cost curve? Savings would be significant and measurable, but they would merely represent keeping the lid on costs. The Japanese producers' sharp decrease in purchased parts costs on a yearly basis intrigued Deere management. If the transplants' supply chain pros—American managers, working in North America with primarily American suppliers—could save billions and still grow and capture more market share with new products and higher volumes, why couldn't Deere?

And the answer was, "Yes you can!"

Optimizing the Supply Chain

In this economy, when some companies save money by cutting back on people and new systems and new initiatives, smart use of resources becomes even more important. It is becoming difficult for a small- or medium-size supplier to do anything but get production out. What initiatives can no company afford to abandon?

Ninety percent of all companies do not take advantage of the cash available from optimizing their supply chain—every day, they let money flow through their fingers. For example, imagine a company called North American Automotive Supplier manufacturing and selling $200 million of product annually, with a total spend of about $100 million.

If this manufacturer's goal is to make a 5 percent after-tax profit, and everything goes well, the company will earn $10 million in a good year. On the company's $200 million in sales, if it puts into place the right capabilities—"enlightened" supply chain professionals who are educated and leveled up to the top quartile, if not higher—the company could easily save 3 to 5 percent a year, every year, of that $100 million spend. (Five percent is not easy, but 3 percent per year is, assuming the company has not done so already—and remember that 90 percent of companies have not done so already.)

The savings accumulate. In year one, the easily achievable 3 percent savings amounts to $3 million of North American's $100 million spend; by year two, it would have totaled $6 million. At this point, purchasing would be finding savings on different parts of the spend, typically, so that by year three, the total still grows, to $9 million. In year four, savings climb to $12 million, and by the fifth year in North American's Spend Management plan, the company would have accumulated a whopping $15 million. In fact, in five years, if the company were to get a handle on the spend using sound verify, track, and control (VTC) principles, North American Automotive's cumulative $15 million in cost savings would represent *50 percent more than its best year's profits!* Retaining another $15 million in spend translates to revenue growth of 7.5 percent sales growth—all without adding any new products or plants!

Look what happened to profitability with a simple 3 percent annual improvement. Amazingly, any good company can achieve 3 percent improvement. When companies aggressively pursue Spend Management, they can increase the goal to 5 percent. For North American Automotive Supplier in our example, a 5 percent after-tax yearly spend savings would mean $5 million per year, or $25 million in five years, again more than double one year's "normal" $10 million profit.

It sounds too good to be true. And in many companies, unfortunately it is. Savings just like these seem to evaporate by the end of the budget cycle—it's not a mystery where the "extra" cash went. We see far too many operations that successfully negotiate new contracts to free up fresh cash, only to lose it to another category of expenditures. Or, when finance fails to monitor the projected savings by reviewing invoices and payments, somehow that well-earned cost reduction seems to disappear. So, savings without tracking is meaningless. We'll talk more later about how to preserve savings by using another element of good Spend Management, the discipline of VTC.

How many companies would like to double their current profit, by using basically their current workforce? If they ratchet up workforce performance and invest in Best Practices and Spend Management, it's an incredibly powerful message. But the single largest problem in all of this smart sourcing is that *people don't believe it*. Senior management personnel have so many things to think about that they look right past Spend Management because it's perceived as "too hard," because it cannot be done in fifteen minutes by the one-minute manager.

Spend Management is a program that takes six or seven and sometimes eight years to execute. Successful supply chains have to build up the capability through their people, systems, and processes, and they have to keep it going. We take the 5 percent savings from two different directions:

1. For 3 percent savings, 50 percent would come from current purchased production parts.

2. The remaining 50 percent comes from supplier integration, working with suppliers' engineering departments in up-front relationships to lower costs as we develop new products together. When producers work side-by-side on new products from the concept stage, we achieve big savings together.

So there are two approaches—Best Practices and Spend Management—to competitive supply management, both directed toward first controlling costs and then growing purchasing capabilities over the long term. Let's look at four different examples of good companies achieving the Incredible Payback.

The Incredible Payback Works for Everyone!

These four stunning examples are good illustrations of The Incredible Payback—Honda, Deere, Delphi, and Respironics. We will continue to look at them as we move through other areas of The Incredible Payback.

HONDA OF AMERICA—1998 ACCORD TOTAL MANUFACTURED COST WAS CUT BY OVER 25 PERCENT

Most automotive producers outsource more than 80 percent of the cost of a vehicle. The percentage of outsourced material contribution to total vehicle cost has been increasing as more vehicle designs call for systems—dashboard systems, seat systems, ignition systems, and even audio systems—rather than five or six thousand individual component parts bought from suppliers and shipped in for component assembly at various feeder lines.

At the same time, customers like Honda and Toyota have reduced the number of suppliers they rely on to produce these subsystems. Honda, for example, used only 353 suppliers to provide all components for its Accord and Civic assembly lines; contrast this very manageable number of suppliers with the thousands of suppliers that auto producers typically used fifteen years ago. Supplier involvement and new model design work allowed Honda buyers to reduce vehicle costs by more than 25 percent.

As producers reduced the number of suppliers with which they partnered, however, they increased the performance demands and reliability/quality expectations for each of these suppliers. Contract totals, as well as the professional level of buyers inside supply management, rose. Honda's procurement department essentially included one well-trained professional for each supplier on the Honda payroll. So what happened in this big shift of purchasing roles and objectives? As the number of suppliers dropped, the need for involvement and expertise around supplier technologies and scheduling rose. Essentially, procurement traded high volumes of day-to-day buying and tracking transactions for fewer high-impact customer/supplier relationship work details—problem-solving design collaboration, for example. The leaders raised the ante for procurement involvement in corporate strategies.

For Honda, the investment in 350 professionals in procurement to support some 350 suppliers yielded not simply high-level day-to-day performance but an Incredible Payback. Honda's strategic sourcing strategy put the company's Accord in neck-to-neck competition with Toyota's similar and competitively priced Camry. Both sedans offered consumers a new price point. Toyota surprised its Marysville competition by reaching 30 percent, a few points above the Accord, cost down in its Camry.

JOHN DEERE & COMPANY

After Deere discovered that its profitability could be greatly improved by adopting some of the excellent supply management practices of the transplants, the company decided to try some new ideas. The company imported key supply management professionals who were familiar with Honda's methods. The company immediately introduced Deere to Best Practices and Spend Management, and the results were encouraging; hundreds of supplier kaizen and lean projects turned in impressive productivity, inventory, and cycle time improvements. The relationship building and integration of new ideas between the customer and eager suppliers strengthened and energized the supply base and prepared teams for more.

In Spend Management, Deere opportunities were abundant, and detailed cost analysis uncovered many opportunities to target cost imbalance in all commodities, starting with big ones like steel, as well as many MRO items. Initial results were so exciting that Deere management was eager for more kaizen and cost target work. Spend Management, however, is more of a long-term discipline than most kaizen work conducted in the supply base, and Deere confirmed this time frame. One of the organization's foundation pieces for long-term sustained Spend Management is a central procurement function that makes all strategic sourcing decisions for the company.

In its first year, Deere strengthened its supply management leadership team and added cost management processes. The payback was $120 million in net savings, enough to cause management to optimistically raise the savings objective from 2.8 percent to 5 percent, an aggressive top-performance level not achieved by more than a handful of healthy organizations.

 A Sample of Deere's Year-One Paybacks:

Projects	Savings
IT Desktop	$7.3M
MRO	3.0
Travel	3.0
Contingent	4.6
Fleet	0.41

Deere's new supply management organization was able to achieve incredible results in five years, more than a $40.5 million reduction in the corporate spend, while plants and divisions continued to have a voice in the sourcing process. Centralization of supply management continued to ensure Deere even bigger gains.

Before	*After*
❑ No consistent strategic sourcing process	❑ Common strategic sourcing process
❑ Unit sourcing authority (maverick spending)	❑ Enterprise/division sourcing based on approved strategies
❑ Volume leveraging covering 15 to 20 percent of spend	❑ Enterprise/division leveraging for 90 percent of spend
❑ Factory-managed supply base (decentralized)	❑ Enterprise/division managed supply base
❑ Inconsistent demands and messages	❑ One face to suppliers

DELPHI CORPORATION'S INCREDIBLE PAYBACK

A few years ago, Delphi Corporation further raised the bar for performance by taking another look at strategic sourcing. While first-tier producers—the Big Three and the transplants—were working at cost management and new product launch challenges, Delphi discovered that second- and third-tier producers had equally formidable challenges. Product variety and complexity continued to grow, as their first-tier customers demanded technology, price, and scheduling successes, one after another. It seemed that the stress of first-tier producers had been magically outsourced to their second- and third-tier suppliers, where the pressure continued to build.

Like many suppliers, Delphi needed new ways to protect profit margins while maintaining healthy growth and the kind of quality and innovation that the market demanded. At Delphi, 59 percent of sales dollars go to purchased goods and services, while 29 percent is spent on manufacturing in-house costs (6 percent for engineering and R&D, and 6 percent for SG&A), which leaves little for profit. To change the equation and produce a predictable and healthy 10 percent profit (or $2.6 billion), Delphi's manufacturing and purchased costs—the biggest cost contributors—had to be reduced considerably over a reasonable horizon of five years. The big question for Delphi management was, however, where the savings would come from.

The answer came from Delphi procurement. Their response was simple—The Incredible Payback. By raising the bar internally on performance, Delphi cut waste and achieved its greatest ever levels of efficiency and productivity. Delphi's lean transformation internally was, in fact, so effective that five plants were awarded the Shingo Prize for their leaned-out processes. Delphi executives knew that taking the same excellent internal performance to outside suppliers would generate even more big savings. Current rates would need to be improved dramatically, while implementing new systems for cost management and model-to-model cost reductions.

Investing in people and systems to generate high paybacks is an absolute requirement. So when Delphi supply managers asked for an additional $25 million a year to invest in high-yield manpower and systems, they knew they would receive $75 million back in savings, or three times their original investment.

In the recession of 2002 to 2003, Delphi's Spend Management and Best Practices created a buzz in Detroit. There was talk of layoffs of ten thousand technical and professional people to cut costs. But why not, suggested one vice president, take another look at Spend Management and look for savings (and new profits) there, particularly in low-cost areas of the world, if the company would put the resources in place to do it? The vice president wanted the company to hire sixty-eight supply chain professionals (engineers and strategic procurement specialists) and they guaranteed that the new hires would realize four times their original $5 million investment, or another $20 million. Furthermore, procurement knew that many parts could be bought for 30 percent less, and the company could double or triple profits in three to five years. Why not try it? Assign a CPO, and give that person 100 percent global buying authority. Sure, it's a grind, but it works! A call to purchasing managers for specific suggestions brought in more than four hundred of them, and the savings rolled in.

Respironics, Inc., a High-Growth Medical Devices Company

Respironics, which has its headquarters in Pittsburgh, Pennsylvania, is a $470 million producer of medical products such as sleep apnea devices and breathing equipment. The company knew its margins were eroding, despite a booming annual 17 percent growth rate and a long series of successful new products. Benchmarking excellent supply chain performers, including Dell, Honda, Harley-Davidson, and IBM, convinced Respironics's executives that a supply management initiative combining Best Practices, especially supplier development, and some Spend Management, would show strong results fast. With a nearly $200 million spend spread over some 1,500 suppliers, the executives knew tremendous opportunities lay untouched in the supply chain, and they were not disappointed.

By creating a new strategic sourcing function, and adding two dedicated professionals to work with costs and supplier development, the company developed a plan designed to show results in a matter of months. A $10 million privately held key plastic face mask supplier was chosen for Respironics's first supplier development project, and as predicted, with a few weeks of training and experienced guidance from Dave Curry, a Honda purchasing veteran, things started to look better, and work better, at this company. Team members picked a team name—TAT for "take action today"—and started to gather baseline data.

"Cardboard Is Not a World-Class Material!"

Those words were uttered by Mark Preston, Respironics's supplier development manager.

For five weeks, Dave Curry's team observed and gathered data, and learned *patience*. As Curry remembers it, team members were, as most kaizen veterans will tell you, eager to get moving and do something. They were new to the data gathering and analysis game, and they wanted to get it over with. "We had to practically strap them to the chairs," recalls Curry, but the results were important because team members were convinced not to attack their first obvious target after studying the numbers.

Respironics needed more production in the hospital face mask area, a product group growing at ever increasing rates. But this key supplier was experiencing 18 percent rejects. So, four Respironics and four supplier process improvement team members got to work and uncovered the following:

Actual	*Goal*
COPDS (5S compliance)	1.12
Volume per day, 2636	3400
Line balance 81.3%	90%
Cycle time 77 seconds	15 seconds
Rejects 18%, or 300/day	200/day, May, 150 or less
Batch	one-piece flow
Wait time on assembly line, 9 sec	5 seconds
Travel distance 527 feet	under 400
Floor space 7153	6500
Inventory, work in process 19K	15K, or 4 to 5 days going to 3 days
Raw material 4K on the floor	3 days

The suggestion system tallied over fifty from the floor in the first four weeks, over half usable.

The team established quantitative goals and picked targets. Among the first objectives included taking one model line from batch to one-piece flow for hospital masks. Reject levels were high at about 18 percent, complicated by a difficult layout and ergonomic challenges. With good margins but too much waste, the company was ripe for transformation, and Curry predicted that the company would double productivity on its first project.

In April, a management review meeting went over the team results. The supplier's insurer toured the plant and was blown away by the change in buildings, equipment, processes, even the way people looked, which was happier and more energetic. They were stunned by the amount and quality of hard data papering the war room's walls, and stated, "We've never seen this type of information at a company this size!"

LOGISTICS.COM

We mentioned the importance of looking at the entire supply chain, from inbound material and purchasing through processing and manufacturing and out to distribution and logistics. The complexity of supply networks delivering on JIT schedules demands lots of very smart software assists, and a few companies have taken advantage of outstanding optimization software to look at their material flows and their spend. Optimization software used by logistics providers and shippers is a great payback opportunity area. Quaker Oats, for example, worked four times with Logistics.com (now part of Manhattan Associates), an optimization software provider. Each time, the company cut an impressive 4 to 8 percent off its transportation spend, saving millions of dollars and improving service levels. Similarly, consumer products giant Fortune Brands, whose brand names include Jim Beam, Knob Creek, Geyser Peak, Titleist, Cobra, Footjoy, Master locks, Moen, Day-Time, Kensington, and

Swingline, saved over $900,000 through a collaborative transportation procurement agreement reached with Logistics.com.

It's an opportunity that purchasing executives cannot overlook.

Conclusion

Honda, Deere, and Delphi—each one of these operations once had traditional purchasing and manufacturing/distribution practices, with low and unpredictable yields. Each of the four had to create a new awareness of procurement's role in driving corporate profits. And each company boasts supply management leaders who continually take the lead in meeting corporate revenue objectives. No longer simply a cost burden, procurement's contributions to the bottom line have won the attention of investors and shareholders alike.

In a desperate economy, when so many companies simply dissolve and others lay off thousands of good employees, smart use of all resources becomes even more important. We said that ordinary performance will give a company from 2 to 3 percent savings in purchased costs; however, more aggressive and thoughtful pursuit of Spend Management and Best Practices guarantees a 3 percent annual savings. But expert application of these two approaches takes a good company into the small group of excellent performers who project and deliver 5 percent savings or more annually.

Raising levels of supply base performance does not come without some upfront investment, however. Deere added 175 new strategic supply management positions: 100 for supplier development, 50 cost management specialists, and 25 Best Practice specialists. Honda of America dedicates approximately four hundred purchasing professionals to strategic sourcing and working with suppliers; the rough payback that Honda calculates on its $100,000 annual investment in a supplier engineer is three to five times the annual salary package, or $300,000 to $500,000 in cost reductions and productivity improvements, which is not a bad payoff!

We believe that to combine short-term results with long-term financial gains, a company must master both approaches to The Incredible Payback—that is, managing the spend and strategic sourcing, combined with Best Practices. Whether the discipline is called kaizen, Honda BP, or lean methods, the combined payoff will be more certain, with less risk, and will provide a solid foundation for growth.

Best Practices pay off. Eighty percent of companies enjoy The Incredible Payback opportunity, but only the best maintain focus to implement more than a few Best Practices in the supply base, or internally in local production or procurement operations. With only partial initiatives, their results may be promising, but they are generally limited and difficult to maintain. Furthermore, few procurement operations are centralized and equipped to carry out high-level Spend Management, the type of hard-driving discipline that yields billions of dollars in savings. Although we are working with different cultures, different size companies, different life cycles, and different tools, every company faces a common challenge—the opportunity to save billions without laying off millions. It can be done!

Notes

1. Dave Nelson, Rick Mayo, and Patricia E. Moody, *Powered by Honda* (New York: John Wiley & Sons, 1999), p. 5.
2. Anthony C. Laraia, Patricia E. Moody, and Robert W. Hall, *The Kaizen Blitz* (New York: John Wiley & Sons, 1999), pp. 3–5.
3. Dave Nelson, Patricia E. Moody, and Jonathan Stegner, *The Purchasing Machine, How the Top Ten Companies Use Best Practices to Manage Their Supply Chains* (New York: The Free Press, 2001), p. 29.
4. Ibid., pp. 45–63.
5. Patricia E. Moody, *Breakthrough Partnering* (New York: John Wiley & Sons, 1993).

Chapter 2

Ten Common Mistakes

TRADITIONAL STRATEGIC AND TACTICAL APPROACHES TO SOURCING, BUILD-ing, and distributing successful products will not allow purchasers to see or capture big paybacks because traditional approaches only provide partial solutions—they don't include Best Practices and Spend Management. Most traditional purchasing and manufacturing functions take a narrow focus that does not reach all key areas of the supply chain; they are not big enough and deep enough to lead the kind of change we envision. Furthermore, since most traditional purchasing organizations' systems are not well-integrated and cannot meet all key information requirements, achieving big paybacks with Spend Management is a challenge. Although it is possible to achieve, year after year, good savings with only limited or partial information, to sustain the 3 to 5 percent total spend savings that we advocate, companies must see the entire spend and they must see beyond this year's budget. Achieving billions of dollars of savings without hurting the supply base or cheating customers out of value is the challenge of every producer, and Best Practices and Spend Management are the answer.

Supply chain risk and uncertainty have arisen as global outsourcing has increased. When companies move more and more of their manufacturing business outside to contract manufacturers, they create more logistics work as materials move through complex supply chains. Many of the hands that touch the materials are not well connected to the end producer, and this also generates more risk that traditional operations are not equipped to handle. As supply networks have become more complex, the risks and the opportunities have arisen as well.

Purchasing processes that limit payback potential include organization structures that conflict or overlap, missing data, and bad practices. Bad practices create waste, which is easy to spot, but capturing and using the right spend data is not as easy to do, and it requires more focused attention. Enterprises that do not maintain a strong focus on Spend Management, which is supported by Best Practices, allow potential paybacks to slip away, and they usually do not know it! Furthermore, the sheer difficulty of data gathering and performance monitoring in traditional operations often obscures the larger vision and goals because managers find themselves sub-optimized by smaller, tactical objectives.

How to Evaluate Your Supply Management Group's Maturity and Competence

There are ten clear pitfalls that limit a supply chain's contribution to profits and growth. These problem areas also mark the difference between mature organizations that are working on all the right issues and bringing along the best resources, and those operations that are stuck in a tactical day-to-day grind.

Before jumping into fixing each of these ten problem areas, however, we recommend that managers perform a quick survey of their operation's capabilities and become familiar with key work areas: understand where procurement people are really spending their time and where there may be gaps. Gene Richter, the former chief procurement officer of IBM, used a thirteen-question check-list to evaluate purchasing performance and to understand what areas are important to the group. This checklist helps to highlight questionable and problem areas and serves as a great starting point for further gap analysis and spend focus. The checklist raises more questions when supply management is reviewed, and it should highlight strengths as well as obvious weaknesses. Use it as a starting point to examine exactly what your company does in the supply chain: where the emphasis is, and where the big dollars are. If your primary area of responsibility is engineering or manufacturing, this checklist will be a perfect jumping-off place for reviewing supply chain operations. These questions are also useful for customer/supplier or engineering/procurement teams to use if they want to streamline their processes, and also to identify and focus on a few important tasks (see Figure 2–1).

---

1. How is procurement organized currently?
   A. Logistics?
   B. Production planning and control?
   C. Incoming material and component quality?
   D. Inventory management?

2. What performance metrics are available currently?
   A. Are they used directly in performance reviews?

3. Who really selects the sources:
   A. Procurement? (Central? Regional? Plant?)
   B. Engineering?
   C. Top management?
   D. If it depends on the commodity, cite some examples.

4. Who negotiates the price and other contract terms?

5. How are make/buy decisions made?
   A. Components?
   B. Finished products?

6. What are the major outside sourced part categories, *based on dollars spent?*

7. What part categories are most critical from a quality, technology, and/or delivery standpoint?

8. Who are the ten most important suppliers? For each, identify:
   A. The primary country of manufacturing origin
   B. The country of headquarters
   C. How often they are visited by procurement people

9. Can your MRP system requirements be:
   A. Cross-communicated within the company?
   B. Consolidated into one demand on the supplier?
   C. Nationally?
   D. Globally?

10. What are company policies regarding:
    A. Ethics
    B. Buyer behavior
    C. Supplier behavior, etc.

11. Are there regular, formal processes for communicating with suppliers and getting their input?
    A. Periodic surveys?
    B. Advisory councils?
    C. Ombudsman?

12. Averages of procurement people:
    A. Years of education?
    B. Predominate discipline?
    C. Years with the company?
    D. Years in procurement?

13. What delegation of financial authority do the various levels of procurement have? Does any other function have procurement delegation authority?

SOURCE: R. Gene Richter, former chief procurement officer, IBM Corporation, copyright 2001, used by permission.

Figure 2–1. Preliminary production procurement questions.

Building on Your Strengths

No purchasing group covers all areas equally well. Harley-Davidson, for instance, works very hard on strategic planning and supplier relationships. Although Honda's purchasing was not strong on computer systems integration, purchasing people worked well with manual data that was accurate and available. We are sure that every group that performs a good management review will find one or two of the most common mistakes made in every supply chain organization. There is not one company that can demonstrate excellent performance in all areas, and very few companies rank above average all around. However, if your group has a few strengths—and some weaknesses—that are important in your industry, we urge you to build on these strengths and see what happens. The ten common mistakes shown in Figure 2–2 are problem areas that we see blocking the progress of far too many good organizations. We think that some, if not all ten, of them can be addressed immediately in ways that will actually change current performance. Before the cure, however, comes diagnosis and treatment.

---

1. Low expectations
2. Decentralized purchasing
3. Production reporting into operations or marketing
4. Lack of good analytical tools
5. Supplier proliferation
6. Short-term, low-level tactical focus
7. Bad press
8. Product variety and complexity
9. No connection or communications between purchasing and new poduct development
10. No supplier development

Figure 2–2.   Ten common mistakes.

Low Expectations

Coauthor Nelson calls this mistake "operating at kindergarten level in a grad school environment," but the practice of allowing purchasing to be an underachiever is an expensive approach to global supply management because it underpowers a vital contributor to corporate profits and growth. Unfortunately, examples of low expectations (and low results) in procurement are common. When compensation and board of director's representation, for instance, does not include supply chain management at high levels, performance suffers. Decisions tend to overlook procurement's contributions to profit, and budgets for staffing and resources in supply management are limited. Or when procurement planners' and managers' compensation is lower than that of managers in other areas, the message is clear: Procurement is an administrative process that makes the wheels turn and keeps the paperwork flowing, but it somehow isn't as professional or important as finance or marketing.

Low expectations make the challenge even more difficult because no matter how good an organization is, no matter how eager its employees are to do their best and to make solid contributions, if the expectations for purchasing's role in the business are low, chances are the results will be the same. High expectations produce high results in sports as well as business; the best athletes in sports such as tennis and golf live with their own internal high expectations, as well as the daily responsibility to stay tops in their rankings, and they know the effect a bad crowd has on the game. When Jimmy Connors and John McEnroe played home matches at the U.S. Open in New York, for example, they both raised their level of game to unexpected heights because the home crowd expected them to play better than ever—and no one was disappointed. But when the U.S. Davis Cup team played hometown favorites like Goran Ivanesevic in Zagreb, Croatia, they suffered painful losses as the crowd cheered their missed hits and booed winners. It made the hill that much steeper and higher to climb. In tennis and golf, mental attitude counts for more than 90 percent of the game; and in new and innovative areas like supply management, attitude and respect count just as much.

SECOND-TIER DOES NOT MEAN SECOND-CLASS

Low expectations can be especially damaging out in the supply base. Many suppliers work hard to deliver perfect quality and on-time performance, but because of their size or clout, they often do not get the respect and appreciation they deserve. It is ironic that as outsourcing places higher and higher proportions of product value in the hands of small- and medium-size suppliers, many first-tier operations still undervalue second- and third-tier contributions.

Second-tier suppliers are often the source of innovation and growth. For first-tier producers, however, 80 percent of the United States' annual new products are developed and produced by second-tier companies. Although these suppliers may not represent the largest portion of a corporate spend, their unique contributions make the supply chain more globally competitive, and that value is beyond measure.

Internally, procurement groups can also suffer from lowered expectations or unclear objectives. We will talk later about what metrics work best to measure supply chain performance. There is great power in numbers; and continued high-level purchasing performance and good press throughout the supply base are the fuel for raising low expectations.

Decentralized Purchasing

Decentralized procurement organizational structures were originally designed to guarantee continuous delivery of plant-specific products directly into factories in order to keep the lines running at all costs. However, they are now our biggest barrier to improved Spend Management, which is a tremendous problem in supply management today. A decentralized purchasing structure is one in which purchasing offices and decision making are not co-ordinated, supplier strategies are not linked, volume is not lever-aged, and relationships exist at low organizational levels and there are local incentive schemes. Although purchasing offices are maintained at the plants or at divisions, there may be a central procurement function as well that performs a few limited procurement functions. Commodity and cost analysis, quality and material specifications, negotiations, buying, strategic planning, and expediting may be conducted at any and all levels and at many different locations in a decentralized organization—and that is the problem. This approach to managing material flows is a legacy of the vertical integration model. Although some elements of that model have shifted as outsourcing and other supply chain flows have moved out, the basic decentralized foundation imprint remains in place in so many corporations that we know it still needs to be addressed at very high levels. Decentralized operations have a tendency also to put one plant in competition with another for the same supplier's work.

Maverick Buying

What happens to the spend, for instance, in a billion-dollar corporation, when every plant maintains its own team of buyers that orders maintenance and repair operations (MRO) materials independently? Because MRO parts and supplies are unglamorous, they are usually overlooked when companies first attempt cost reductions. However, MRO is one of the easiest opportunity areas starting out. As John Deere discovered when a planner studied the company's MRO spend, the result was $1.4 million for 424 different varieties of gloves, all intended to be used on the production floor for basically the same purpose, before being discarded. When the glove supplier mentioned to one Deere analyst that Deere was paying $7.50 for a single-use pair of gloves, while the competition paid $1.50, and then cleaned and reused the gloves, the facts hit home—decentralized spend decisions not only encouraged maverick buying but also increased the cost! By switching to a more-sensible buying strategy that included a single supplier, fewer varieties of gloves, and better prices, planners realized immediate savings of 35 percent, *or $490,000, almost half a million dollars in gloves alone!* Even Deere suppliers knew that lack of control bred inefficiencies! If that type of variance existed for one simple production item, how much craziness would Deere find with bigger items like tires and engine components?

The issue of cost effectiveness is key in any decentralized operation, but there are other problems as well. For suppliers that may be shipping materials to customers at more than one plant, at different prices or specifications, the customer is not showing what Honda calls "same face," which is a uniform approach to buying and communications that minimizes confusion and saves time. Quality specifications may differ from one plant to another, even from one engineer to another, and when the purchasing system allows product or design proliferation, or when there is not an integrated central database to tell the story, no one is the wiser. In a growth company launching many new products each year, this is a problem;, but in a mature industry that earns predictable revenues on a known set of products, it is inexcusably expensive.

Curious Incentives to Stay Decentralized

The centralization/decentralization decision, however, is more than a simple choice based on good analysis of the spend, cost benefits, and production demands. There is strong emotion surrounding the question of whether to decentralize—how much or how fast—and where there is emotion, there is usually power or money. These two issues must be addressed when companies consider how to best structure the supply management area: cost allocation for a central procurement department and the division or plant manager's incentive to retain purchasing power.

First, it costs money to maintain a central purchasing operation, especially when it is staffed by planners who are paid more at central planning than if they were working at the plant level. Central procurement operations require good data from an integrated purchasing system, and this system will probably cost more than smaller plant-level operations. The funding to operate a central system comes from allocations placed on the plants or the division. In essence, the plants pay for planning, negotiating, and buying by a central group that leverages the combined size of all the smaller plants and divisions, while making buys that ideally should work to the advantage of all parties involved. Therefore, there may be a trade-off between the central group's ability to leverage the buy and the plant's contribution to the cost of the central group.

FAIR IS FAIR

When a certain market or group experiences sudden market downturns and no longer needs or can afford its allocation to the central group, there must be an agreement already in place that reduces the purchasing expense, not necessarily staff (sometimes staff can be reallocated to other businesses or product lines that are growing) at headquarters or at the plant level. If the central operation doesn't agree to "share the pain"—sometimes the central staff has the resources to "save the day" that one plant alone couldn't muster—then why should plants choose to delegate this critical operation to them?

"BUT WE'RE SPECIAL, WE'RE DIFFERENT"

A second issue that is raised as a quiet objection is often veiled in the "but we're different" argument. When plants are staffed to expedite or pull in materials and to coordinate shipping schedules with suppliers—not to negotiate spend agreements and buy—the plant manager or division head will have fewer high-paid professionals reporting to him. Would you rather be in charge of production supported by a few planners for $80,000 a year or an entire operation staffed at the plant level with buyers, planners, negotiators, expeditors, and purchasing engineers at $150,000 a year plus management perks? It's easy to see why plant and division managers will fight a central procurement approach if it means their jobs are narrowed to simply production and expediting!

The trade-offs between a central and a decentralized structure become clear, however, when companies look at The Incredible Payback opportunities that appear when purchasing is centralized or centrally managed and controlled. It is interesting to note that Honda is centralized in North America but decentralized globally. It's reasonable to leave expediting and daily material flow in the hands of the plants and the divisions who are responsible for just-in-time performance, but like all other key functions of the business—finance, marketing, and human resources—procurement needs to be centralized to leverage the buy. When just-in-time and excellent supplier quality and delivery performance guarantee predictable material flows, it makes even more sense to move procurement planning, negotiating, and buying operations out of the processing plants.

The question extends beyond pure cost effectiveness to communications, morale, creating technology advantage, and building high-level relationships with supplier partners. The plants should have their processes pretty well nailed, with the exception of emergencies. They should put Spend Management and preservation of intellectual capital where it belongs, at the heart of the corporation, where all corporation spend information is consolidated and available.

Furthermore, a halfway solution—some planning and buying at central, as well as scattered throughout the plants and division—is no solution at all. Redundancy in multiple purchasing staffs is expensive, and

❏ Information sharing and strategic roll ups, vital for The Incredible Payback, are difficult to obtain in decentralized operations

❑ "Some central–some local" encourages maverick buying, a
   Pandora's box that takes years to put back in order

Production Reporting into Operations or Marketing

When significant percentages of corporate spend are outsourced—in the automotive industry the outsourced percentage
can easily reach 85 percent of the total, in the computer industry it
is even higher—it makes good financial sense for all material production and flow functions (in-house and outsourced) to report
into one responsibility center managed by procurement. That is
where costs and supplier performance can be compared and consolidated (see Figure 2–3).

For most companies, the idea of manufacturing reporting to
supply management is a radical concept, the very opposite of traditional practice. In the old production model, purchasing reports
to either operations or product marketing; procurement under
this model has limited reach and limited responsibility as a cost
center that serves production or product divisions. This traditional
operating structure automatically creates waste in several ways.

First, when procurement reports into marketing and serves
product marketing divisions, there is a tendency to grow the parts
lists and create overlap and redundancy, a problem that builds
complexity. When introduction and management of a product
portfolio takes precedence over careful review of the parts lists, it's
easy to accumulate obsolete components that were specified for
one product, but left out of the Bill of Material for the next one. If
purchasing has the ability to consolidate and review Bill of Material data, including supplier preferences, specifications, and pricing, they will of course inevitably catch redundant parts. They may
also, especially if procurement engineers get involved, see parts
that have been "over-spec'd," components that may be requested
at higher or tighter technical specifications than truly required for
acceptance price and feature performance.

Opportunities =
Time, Quality, Cost, Flexibility

Figure 2–3. The manufacturing continuum.

The second organization fallout problem comes when purchasing reports to production or operations. Companies that still live with this model neglect Spend Management and strategic procurement planning in favor of expedites and other tactical short-term activities. A test of that trend is to review premium freight charges; if they are frequent and high, production is using purchasing as a big expeditor rather than as a partner in profit creation.

When nonpurchasing professionals make purchasing decisions—for example, whether to outsource a critical part—supply chain spend or technology objectives are often overlooked. The growth of the outsourced electronics industry illustrates this point. Initially, companies like IBM sought to outsource difficult or expensive work to board shops that had gathered the right equipment and expertise to make production managers' lives a little easier. Outsourcing made sense, because it simplified the lives of manufacturing executives. The decision to outsource was usually made by manufacturing managers who worried less about the cost of materials and more about the availability of supply. The make/buy decision was simple because electronics suppliers always priced their products lower than what original equipment manufacturers (OEMs) could do themselves, and they guaranteed delivery. But gradually, the financials started to turn the other way as contract suppliers learned more about component prices than their customers. Customers lost visibility to parts prices. As contract manufacturers took more control of component specification or deliveries, many of them found ways to make more money on component prices than processing, and their OEM customers lost the ability to manage component suppliers well or profitably. A simple decision to outsource production headaches grew into a blind spot, a cash drain that procurement managers find difficult to reverse.

Lack of Good Analytical Tools

Even when traditional ERP and other procurement software solutions do not offer the kind of simple analytics required to identify and realize high payback solutions, it is essential for Spend Management to find other solutions that allow good analysis. There are many creative solutions, clever ways to get around the lack of good data; some solutions are short-term, one-time data-gathering and analysis projects, while others can be tacked on to the larger procurement or accounting software. What is essential for profitable Spend Management is the ability to gather, consolidate, manipulate, and analyze procurement information from many sources. The frequency of analysis at minimum should be once per quarter.

Many large organizations with multiple databases find it difficult to consolidate key Bill of Material data. Deere's "one intern and a spreadsheet" story offers one solution to the problem of missing analytics: Deere wanted to understand how much steel, what types, and at what prices the company was buying all over the world. Management sensed that there were opportunities to leverage the buy and achieve multimillion dollar savings in steel, as well as in other commodities. However, it was impossible to gather accurate information from all of Deere's steel plants around the world. Different Deere buyers operated under different decentralized policies, so it was hard to obtain the correct information from each one. The solution was to hire a central purchasing intern who, over a period of two to three months, was able to retrieve accounts payable data that filled in the gaps. The best source for actual payment history was, of course, accounts payable for tracking purchase orders back to negotiated contract prices, which is another checkpoint where potential savings usually lie hidden. Purchasers can review individual contracts or release paperwork, or, as a last resort, they may ask the supplier! For a single high-value commodity like steel, data digging to find cost variance or errors is a worthwhile exercise; trying to capture savings on all commodities, all the time, however, requires consistent and fully centrally integrated data.

Supplier Proliferation

Let's think about the image of a lean supply base. In the old manufacturing days, a factory of five to ten thousand workers was a good thing—bigger was better. Today, optimum factory size is a few hundred personnel. And it's the same with suppliers. In the past, more was better, while today, lean—in the factory and the supply chain—is better.

Customers cannot effectively manage more than three hundred to four hundred key suppliers. Supplier proliferation dilutes an organization's focus, and eliminates the type of in-depth technology and commodity intelligence development that is required to meet high levels of quality and price performance. A surplus of suppliers also limits the number of high-level partnerships that good relationship builders can develop, and it makes supplier development too expensive to undertake on a large scale. We are not recommending single sourcing all commodities, however, an approach that carries great risk, particularly for North American operations with global networks. We do find, in fact, that purchasing groups that have deliberately reviewed and narrowed down their supply base to a manageable number will be able to gather and apply Best Practices and Spend Management initiatives much more successfully because they are starting from a good position. Decentralized procurement unfortunately builds supplier proliferation, and when organizations want to bring all buying and negotiation activities into one central point, they will need a method to review and reduce, or rationalize, the supply base at the same time. Sometimes, the supplier historical data will show slightly better performance for one supplier whose price is higher than the others. The value of good performance data is that performance/cost trade-offs will be clearer and easier to see. In terms of payback, focusing development resources on a few selected and clearly high-potential suppliers makes more financial sense than scattering attention over several hundred suppliers of unknown potential.

Short-Term, Low-Level Tactical Focus

If supply management visibility is high only when a hot order appears, production is in jeopardy, or if the floor screams for premium expedites, tactical focus will continue to obscure higher level objectives. In a tactical operation, it is difficult to achieve payback without beating up suppliers, which is an approach that cannot be successfully sustained. Suppliers will run for the nearest exit plan! A tactical focus tends to eat up resources at the plant level, and it sometimes has an impact on central procurement as well. A reasonable approach to strategic versus tactical focus is to escalate emergency or chronic plant procurement issues—such as bad quality or poor deliveries—to central purchasing where a supplier's overall performance can be reviewed at the contract level. However, when an organization is mired in daily problems and planning horizons that barely stretch through lead time, it is nearly impossible to impose strategic work on top of the daily grind.

We think far too many companies still expend dedicated resources on short-term fire fighting, and that imbalance signals either bad supplier selection, poor communications, or very unpredictable plant production schedules. All these issues are solvable, but they must be addressed at the proper level.

Bad Press

We need to learn a lesson from marketing, and then use it everyday. Strategic sourcing speaks the language of management—financials such as profit and loss (P&L), expenses, and contributions are the buzzwords that top management wants to hear about, the ones that purchasing professionals need to emphasize in all their communications. When procurement executives do not make the clear and direct connection between their contribution to profitability and revenue growth, they relegate themselves to cost areas that always cry for cuts. It's a tough, reactive position to be in. To reverse this bad reputation, procurement professionals must turn their image around to reflect a positive one of profit and value creation. Reliance on savings and cost cutting to the exclusion of growth and improvement, as both GM and Chrysler learned in the 1990s, creates bad press and loses good suppliers, which is a difficult trend to reverse. Remember that your work is known to both inside press (your peers, top management, and your people) as well as to outside press (*Purchasing* magazine, *Supply Management*, *Fortune* magazine, and the *New York Times*). Remember that bad press is difficult to reverse, but no press is a great opportunity to mine. The Tylenol poisoning case in which President James Burke communicated a strong message that told the world McNeil (a Johnson & Johnson company) had itself also been hurt, and that the company planned to refill the pipeline with tamper-proof products, saved the company and established a benchmark for how to deliver bad news well. Burke's good press position put Johnson & Johnson in a better recovery position as well.

Product Variety and Complexity

Chrysler discovered in the 1980s that a focus on product variety carried down to the level of piece parts, nuts and bolts, and screws, could bankrupt the company. Unfortunately, many procurement groups inherit a long line of unnecessary parts selected generations earlier by individual buyers and engineers. Although these buyers had little idea of the exact financial impact of their selections, today most planners are aware that complexity costs.

John Deere's glove story illustrates the pitfalls of unlimited parts proliferation. Theresa Metty, chief procurement officer at Motorola, believes that parts proliferation and complexity is one of sourcing's biggest challenges. She has launched a "War on Complexity" that emphasizes elimination of excess parts to the tune of several million dollars. Simplifying, or rationalizing, the parts list is a long-term solution that has immediate payback. If producers want to find immediate cost relief and change the way buyers and engineers work together, reduction of variety and complexity is a great place to start.

Purchasing Separate from New Product Development

When Gene Richter headed up Hewlett Packard's purchasing group, his dream was to have "a buyer at every engineer's elbow," and his hope was that an integrated management information system (MIS) would provide the design and price information that both departments needed. Nearly twenty years later his dream remains unrealized, and one solution has been to physically colocate supply management with new products engineers.

Both Honda and Delphi have found that establishing stronger links between purchasing and engineering or R&D earlier in the cycle are critical to optimizing this upfront area of the supply chain.

Another key systems issue that helps to achieve functional integration is the lack of a Bill of Material database accessible to both areas offering the kind of information that engineers as well as planners and buyers require. Previously, engineering did not see contract information, such as pricing, that purchasing worked with. In a robust system environment, however, all design and pricing information, as well as supplier performance history, is readily available to all authorized users. Although new product development engineers may be based in Detroit, Tokyo, Berlin, or wherever, planners and buyers can be located in Hungary or Indonesia, China or Mexico, and the information still hangs together well.

No Supplier Development

Perfect performance—zero rejects and perfect on-time delivery for every part—is achievable at all levels of the supply chain, but it is unusual. Each spring, Honda of America fetes its excellent suppliers with recognition awards that prove error-free performance is possible. But, for every Nippondenso, a multiple award winner, and Johnson Controls' excellent track record, there are dozens of suppliers who need technology and management assistance to reach higher levels. Usually supplier development engineers are a resource that customers can more easily provide than small- and medium-size suppliers, at least to get started. The range of assists needed by suppliers to achieve high levels of quality and performance is long, from quality circles and supplier seminars, where new ideas are explored, to SWAT team rapid response assistance in emergencies. Supply chain organizations that do not include people who can work with suppliers at the plant level are missing big savings and performance opportunities. The proven payback for supplier development personnel is three to four times their cost, and this investment is one that is quickly paid back but most frequently overlooked.

The Fear Factor

All these ten items require significant change: new policies, new measurements, and new strategies for every commodity. It seems that even tackling one or two obstacles brings up new problems to solve. There are many reasons why companies naturally encounter resistance to change, such as fear of job loss, fear of having to learn new processes, or fear of having to move to another area. Fear is a powerful inhibitor that can sometimes serve a useful purpose, but when good companies are attempting to make reasonable changes using proven methods, fear just gets in the way.

Amazingly, when we describe the "before" and "after" views of improved supply management operations, especially in Spend Management dollars, everyone is energized. When we relate case examples of real companies like Honda and Delphi and their suppliers, which have instilled a culture of continuous improvement and change, people become believers.

Yet, despite the promise of better work and bigger opportunities to come, fear remains. Some statistics from a book by David Ropeik, director of risk communication at the Harvard Center for Risk Analysis, highlight the apparent craziness of acting in fear of change. The list of things we fear is long, and growing—spiders, snakes, smallpox, anthrax, airplane crashes, terrorism, credit card debt. However, the odds of dying before the average age of eighty from unnatural causes are not as high as we fear. The risk of dying in a plane crash is one in 9 million; being killed by lighting is one in 3 million; dying in a flood, one in almost 7 million. Our fear of events over which we have no control, such as airplane crashes, is stronger than our fear of problems we can prevent. One of the most common and preventable killers, heart disease, has earned a probability of one in three hundred, yet Americans are notorious for bad diet and sedentary lifestyles that inevitably cause health problems.[1]

Fear is a strange motivator. The immediate threat can be more important than the imagined and less probable ones. The lesson for companies and teams contemplating change is to understand and expect that fear will accompany change. The best approach is to recognize and acknowledge the resistance, and move quickly into realistic and profitable challenges at hand. Once the first problem has been resolved, team members can more quickly move to the next one.

Sense of Adventure

If you want to pick up big savings fast, and more later on, if you are not satisfied with traditional procurement's predictable yearly price increases of 3 to 7 percent, and you are willing to take on the work of major organizational change, then you are ready to begin The Incredible Payback. If your heroes are purchasing giants like Honda, Delphi, and Toyota—market makers that return profits through procurement—then you are ready to begin. You know the old ways won't get you there, so are you ready to make some money?

Note

1. David Ropeik, *Risk: A Practical Guide for Deciding What's Really Safe and What's Really Dangerous in the World Around You* (Boston: Houghton Mifflin, 2002).

Chapter 3

How to Build a Fair Advantage and Capture The Incredible Payback

On Focus—"Tennis is an unforgiving sport that requires focus and 'getting ready,' lots of preparation. In fact, preparation to serve is as important as throwing the ball up and hitting through. If the server can imagine his target spot, take a deep breath, exhale and 'see' the target, the ball will go in. It's about *focus.*"

—Avis Murray, two-time winner of Sr. Women's Masters Cup

No two companies, products, or suppliers are alike, but they all need a set of common foundation blocks, basic data points that mark the journey, before they can begin to realize their full potential and move up to the next performance level. Focusing on the target—that is, "seeing the objective"—is important all the way throughout the change (see Figure 3–1). Supply management organizations that grew from traditional order placement and expediting groups will find that moving up to The Incredible Payback requires change on many fronts, including learning how to partner

70

Building our Supply Management Capabilities

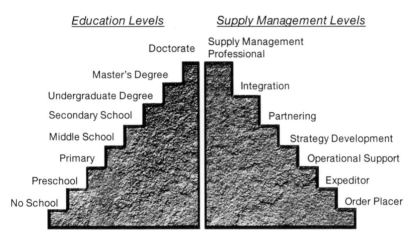

Figure 3-1. Supply management capabilities.

with suppliers, integrating with other functions, and strategic sourcing.

By using this list of ten Bad Practices to perform a preliminary review of your group, you will discover where your company has weaknesses and where traditional practice is holding you back. If your organization can answer yes to more than three of these ten traditional practices, your performance will be limited. If you want to deliver strong paybacks for the company's purchasing investment, it will be necessary to rebuild the procurement function:

1. The highest level of purchasing executive is the purchasing manager.
2. Buyers/planners earn less than one-third of the highest purchasing professional's compensation package.
3. The board of directors includes vice presidents of marketing, finance, and manufacturing, but no representatives of the supply chain.
4. Strategic alliances are guaranteed by long written contracts.

5. New product development expertise is centered in engineering.
6. Planning systems in purchasing are connected loosely—or not at all—to MRP/ERP and other manufacturing planning and execution software.
7. Supplier delivery schedules are derived from faxed requirements.
8. Compensation of purchasing professionals is based solely on purchased price variance cost data.
9. Point of consumption deliveries of certified materials represents 10 percent or less of all receipts.
10. Measuring product quality by commodity and part classification is the responsibility of manufacturing.

These ten questions represent a good starting point for change agents to quickly review a supply chain to find the weak spots and strengths and to gauge its financial capabilities. It is important to identify big problem areas and to prioritize the ones that will be changed first. When companies customize the basics to fit their own challenges and their own extended supply chains, the result will be even stronger and more resistant to problems.

Once supply management has taken a quick look at capabilities, the next step is to look at four strategic areas that will reveal either opportunities or problem spots. These following four areas are vital to creating The Incredible Payback because they describe the relationship between the customer and its suppliers in the extended enterprise:

1. Cost Management
2. Report card on supplier quality and delivery
3. Evaluation of suppliers' technological capabilities
4. Wavelength—a subjective evaluation of how well companies align, or work together, and mesh their cultures

The first of four areas that needs to be looked at for The Incredible Payback is Cost Management. In order to understand Cost Management a company needs to take a hard look at what is being spent and with whom. This includes the entire network of suppliers—internal and external—that provide materials, labor, and services like travel, health benefits, and even temporary workers. Cost Management includes spend analysis and Spend Management.

Everything that appears in the income statement as a cost, whether it is cost of goods sold (including manufacturing processes, outsourced contract manufacturing, and materials) or overhead and administrative expenses, is part of the company's spend, the figure that is subtracted from revenues to show what remains—that is, profit before taxes. It is important to note that every dollar that a company spends to make and sell product eventually reduces profit before earnings, and from this number comes the profit margin percentage that tells whether a company is working hard and earning profits or simply working hard and covering costs. For growth and shareholder returns, we want to see companies keep that cost figure at least in line with the industry average, or better.

For instance, if we look at the white goods segment of the appliance industry, we will probably see profit margins in the 1 to 4 percent range, lower than what we would see in children's toys, where profit margins as well as risk can be astronomical. We won't deal here with tax liabilities or how much tax your earnings generate, we are only concerned with all the hundreds of items that subtract from the sales figure.

We can tie the impact of the purchasing spend directly to profitability because all the funds spent by purchasing, even for capital equipment, are deducted from revenues.

Let's look again at the income statement of the imaginary automotive supplier, Allied Auto, to see how purchasing fits into the income statement:

Revenue from sales	$2.5 billion
Cost of goods sold:	
Cost of purchased goods and services	
(55 percent of sales)	$1.375 billion
Manufacturing in-house (33 percent of COGS)	$ .825 billion
Engineering and R & D (6 percent)	$ .15 billion
SG & A (Selling, General and Administrative)	
(6 percent)	$ .15 billion
Profit	0

Allied shareholders are not happy with their zero yield, and the chairman believes it's time to start making a profit. He would like to see a solid 10 percent margin, or $.25 billion over five years, and that means another half billion dollars should be added to the coffers each year. The board of directors agrees, but its members aren't specific about how to generate this big increase in profits.

What are Allied's choices? We said in Chapter 1 that the first and most obvious, and clearly least realistic step, is to simply raise prices by 10 percent across the board. Next possibility, and one that is equally unattractive, requires steep cuts, with plant closings and big layoffs, enough to produce $.25 billion dollars of savings. The trouble with this option is that it's a one-time event and gutting the company will deprive it of the ability to respond to market upswings or to make new product launches. Laying off engineers and other technical staff, such as buyers and commodity experts, will cut into the company's stream of innovation producers, its R&D department. Is there any other possible source of a half billion dollars a year in savings that would be enough to fund the current production rate and more?

That's where The Incredible Payback comes in. By far the biggest segment of product costs lies in the $1.375 billion line item for the purchasing spend. A 10 percent savings here, the chairman's annual target, would represent only 3.6 percent of the total annual spend.

Savings Levels

We've said that most average, traditional purchasing opera-tions can, without too much difficulty, cut their spend by 1 to 2 percent, just by paying closer attention to how they buy. We call this the beginner's level, and it does not require big organizational changes or significant investment to earn 1 percent savings. Sug-gestion systems and some supply base consolidation can easily yield a 1 percent savings (see Figure 3–2).

Intermediate and Expert Level Savings

Companies that use some of our Best Practices can achieve from 3 to 5 percent in savings, year after year, with steady attention to basics and continuous improvement. Going above 5 percent savings year after year is aggressive, and best suited for expert sup-ply chain groups with high-performance suppliers, excellent com-munications, and very responsive operations; those who are the best of the best.

Allied Automotive finds itself in the middle performance area,

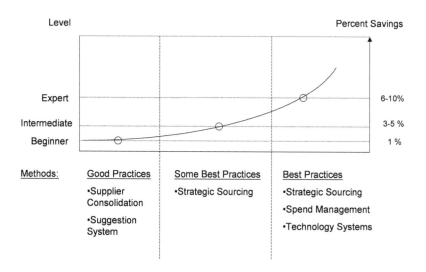

Figure 3–2. Three levels of savings.

challenged to meet and maintain the goal. Year one is easy pick-
ings; simply by reviewing the number of suppliers, consolidating,
and dropping more costly sources, the deed is done. Next, purchasing attacks some supplier problems causing late deliveries
and quality rejects; supplier development costs money, although it
is a guaranteed investment. This is where most good intentions fall
to the wayside because it takes more than good suppliers and best
practices to build an operation that can consistently deliver a
string of high-percentage savings. Companies such as Honda and
Toyota have proven they can meet these aggressive goals and even
exceed them, but for most traditional operations, after the low
hanging fruit is gone, things become difficult.

So Allied Automotive, an enlightened and lean operation,
wants to take the high road. Surprisingly, the purchasing director
raises his hand. "It's not such a hard thing," he volunteers, "because I know we can eliminate 2.5 to 3 percent costs in the value
stream. We can easily get 3 percent from supplier internal continuous improvements. Internally, we have a 2 percent goal on some
material cost improvements—for instance, we're trying to do standardization. Bingo, that makes 5 percent, and we know we can get
that final 1 percent in our sleep!" Six percent shaved off the purchasing spend sounds like a very attractive contribution to the
chairman's 10 percent objective. The board is slightly disbelieving,
but it's desperate to hear a positive scenario.

"This doesn't come for free, however," the purchasing vice
president warns, as she prepares the CEO for a few budget requests to meet the savings goals, including a calculated investment to hire supplier development and planning pros, plus some
new smart systems. "We promise you that if you invest, the payback is three-fold. We'll make about 1.5 times on your investment
the first year, and then three times your investment the next year,
and each year thereafter."

So Allied is leveraging purchasing to achieve corporate profitability. It is certainly easier than shutting plants, or launching a

few thousand new products, or dropping sales or manufacturing costs to zero. To move Allied from the intermediate procurement performance level to an expert level, however, will take high performance on all basic areas: Cost Management, supplier performance, and technology assists.

The Foundation: Building on the Basics

These four basic building blocks must be in place before any supply chain can proceed to tougher payback challenges. First, the company must consider the Cost Management numbers. Amazingly, most companies do not know how much they pay for purchased materials and services, nor even from whom they buy, or how much is used by individual divisions or regions. Somehow, the money goes out and product rolls in, but no single person or system understands the flows and aggregate totals.

Until recently, John Deere did not know how much the company spent worldwide on steel! To produce meaningful aggregate numbers, a summer intern researched steel buys from accounts payable files and other manufacturing records. The results filled a deep spreadsheet program. Naturally this one-shot approach is not a permanent solution, but as a valuable piece of spend analysis, it freed up cash to work on other opportunity areas. Other companies rely on their ERP systems to produce the right data, but if they have not succeeded in total system implementation—and many companies have abandoned or reined in their ERP implementations—they will find it hard to reconstruct the right data.

Many organizations, however, show strengths in only one or two of the building blocks; they may have overlooked the others or not had the right resources to address all of them equally well. This is especially true in large decentralized operations that "grew like topsy." Sometimes, we find purchasing buyers working with great supplier technology capabilities information but only partial cost data. Occasionally we find excellent cost history, but there are problems with supplier relationships. It is better to start with all four elements in place, and build from there to address specific components of each. Although a company may want to focus on specific tactical issues, such as on-time delivery, it must maintain strengths on four fronts and address daily problems as they come up.

This is where a fresh set of eyes can truly help a company focus on what is value building and important for the long-term, because without all four of these foundation blocks in place, a company may be able to obtain great results one time, but showing consistent and predictably high results over and over requires all four strengths: Cost Management, a report card on supplier quality and delivery, an evaluation of suppliers' technological capabilities, and wavelength—a subjective evaluation of how well companies align, or work together and mesh their cultures.

Essentially, these four building blocks represent the basic data that everyone needs to partner well and grow a strong extended enterprise. Cost Management allows buyers to answer the following questions: How much does this part cost? How much should it cost? Where is the market going? Are we paying more than everybody else? Step number two, a report card on supplier quality and delivery, is essential for setting goals and making a transition from tactical daily problem solving to the kind of high-level partnering that can only work when suppliers are clearly performing well in quality and delivery areas. The only way to understand quality and delivery performance, and to begin strengthening weak areas, is to start with sound aggregate and detailed performance history. Step number three, an evaluation of a supplier's technological capabilities, is a look into the future—not only is it important to spend the time that planners need to understand where a commodity or a market is moving along the technology continuum, and how expert the supplier is at leading the way, but a thorough grounding in how well a supplier performed with current technologies is a good indicator of where they will be three, four, or five years down the road.

Finally, the seemingly subjective fourth building block of wavelength, or alignment, is a very important indicator of how well people work together: Are they communicating in the same language? Do they handle priorities with the same urgency? Can a supplier grow with a customer? and most important, Do we trust them? This fourth building block includes so many variables that it may seem difficult to measure and therefore difficult to control, but many excellent partners, such as Harley-Davidson, have found that when they address specific partnering issues and work at improvements, they can improve the alignment of the companies in many critical areas.

Let's take a closer look at the four building blocks and some examples of Best Practice companies that have mastered them.

Building Block #1: Cost Management

What if your purchasing manager wanted to award 80 percent of all stamping business to a single supplier that met all foundation requirements but never quite hit cost targets? Would this not be a great loss for both potential partners?

Management changes in even the best suppliers can reverse good partnerships, as one big automotive supplier recently learned. Although its air-conditioning systems supplier had always met all foundation requirements for quality, delivery, cost, technical capability, and even wavelength, everything changed when a new president took over. On a single air-conditioning assembly the supplier raised prices over 15 percent. Because just-in-time systems do not encourage warehousing to preserve old prices, the customer found negotiation and renegotiation of prices to be the only short-term solution. But under new leadership the supplier negotiated in bad faith, and then reneged on the agreement, leaving the customer no choice but to temporarily bring the parts back in-house and look for another global supplier on the same wavelength. The cost to the customer to in-source these parts was $18 million; however, the cost to the supplier was $50 million!

Beyond clear data showing total spend by commodity, price, or key parts, most companies unfortunately don't really know how much purchased parts cost their suppliers to make, process by process, so they can't make the right decisions. Japanese purchasing groups and transplants, however, work hard to develop this in-depth information, so they usually know better than the producers exactly what each step costs. This type of Cost Management detailed expertise works to everyone's advantage, because it eliminates surprises, improves customer/supplier discussions, and allows the experts to focus on key cost segments of part production.

Cost Management information is not intended, however, to deprive suppliers of their fair profit margin. One automotive purchasing vice president uses the following example to illustrate this point: If I came to you and offered to sell you a brand-new Ford Taurus, fully loaded, with plush leather seats and a premium sound system for $150,000, you would walk out of the show room, because you'd know that the price was ridiculous! But it if weren't your money and you didn't care about the price tag, or if that baby was the only car available, despite the ridiculous price tag, the sale might just happen! Traditional operations often buy materials without really knowing the cost, and as time passes, even though the price may escalate, they manage to remain clueless. It's not that uncommon!

Understanding exactly what commodities or parts are supplied around the world by which suppliers, and at what prices and quantities, is the fist step toward rationalizing the relationships, from the ones that may develop that capability over time to the ones who clearly won't be around for the long term. Cost Management information assumes a simple and clear rationale: If a customer knows what a part costs, he will be less likely to pay too much. Furthermore, good data sets a foundation for further cost reductions through value-added engineering activities, in current product as well as on new models.

Opportunities for cost savings abound throughout the extended enterprise, from taking waste out of supplier processes to improving logistics and distribution networks, cutting down transportation costs, and even reducing budgets spent on indirect materials.

THE TOYOTA/DENSO/HONDA MODEL

We like to see supplier selection decisions made using the Toyota/Denso/Honda model of supply base consolidation. One hundred suppliers, a manageable number, should represent 80 to 90 percent of the direct material spend. This approach limits price and performance variance because it allows planners and supplier development engineers to maximize their effort on a predictable number of good partners. The goal is to retain a small group of core suppliers, and another slightly larger group of good performers.

Traditional thinking treats Cost Management as a purchasing function whose main activity is to maintain, track, and negotiate the best prices, and perhaps build awareness of cost trends during market swings. That is an essential buying activity that every company wants to do well, of course, but Cost Management is so much more than that—it is a key ingredient in the kind of Spend Management that delivers long-term payback with no pain. Japanese auto producers have raised Cost Management to a fine science built on deep and specific knowledge of every single process as well as labor and raw material costs. Very early in the new product concept discussion, Japanese and transplant buyers gather cost information to model a new product's target price. They can, in fact, back into projected profits on a new vehicle by targeting costs against an ideal selling price, and then make the numbers and the engineering specs work, with no surprises. Toyota has taken big chunks out of its Camry designs this way, as has Honda with its Accord. And more important, they know how much it should cost their suppliers in material, labor, and even overhead to produce a specific part.

Cost Management is a tremendous challenge that is not necessarily built on massive computerized data generation and analysis but rather on detailed expert knowledge of a specific process or market. IBM takes a similar, intensely numbers-driven approach. IBM's procurement professionals, for example, became experts at tracking and beating market cost trends because their performance and compensation depends on beating the markets. In fact, IBM commodity teams are force-ranked against each other to encourage each commodity team to be the best.

Target costing is the discipline of projecting specific cost points, all the way from product development through full production. Aids to hitting the target accurately are cost tables, detailed data developed on each component, broken down into the cost of material used by a supplier, added to which is the cost of labor, tooling, and other items.

Building Block #2: A Report Card on Supplier Quality and Delivery

A second foundation data requirement is a good report card on supplier quality and delivery, a company's technical capability, and how well the supplier has been able to maintain high quality and delivery performance over time. Consistency counts because as an indication of the robustness of production processes, it is a great predictor (see Figure 3–3).

When purchasers want to narrow a supply base down to focus on a few key suppliers, and when they want to understand how performance in the two key areas of quality and delivery impact product costs, they need a solid supplier history. Furthermore, any kind of supplier development project—from helping with systems

SUPPLIER DEVELOPMENT (SD): KEY TOOL

- SD is more than cost reduction on a part:

  —Costs out of *processes*

  —Mutual benefit

  —Supplier integration

  —Respect and Trust

- *Attitude is KEY*

Figure 3–3. Supplier development: key tool.

integration to taking waste out of a stamping process—begins with a detailed evaluation of just how good this producer is in the top areas of quality and delivery. Are there never any delivery or quality emergencies, are they a regular routine, or might there be clusters of problems coming from increased schedule demands, too many changes, or other numbers that indicate where potential glitches will rack up costs (and chaos!). The only way to understand what is happening in a process is to observe it before studying the numbers. Dorian Shainin, the quality guru and winner of the Shewhart Award, taught us, "Let the numbers lead you," and they will!

Ideally, data covering several years of detailed quality and delivery performance should be available. A minimum three-year history is essential to cover market swings and variances caused by specific problems. Buyers want to understand how well the supplier has been able to maintain high quality and delivery performance over time, and how quickly the supplier can identify and fix problems. Consistency counts because it is a great predictor of the robustness of production processes.

Supplier quality information must contain clues for problem

solving, as well as tracking. For instance, quality data includes first-time quality, rejects and reworks/total pieces tried, warranty data, part validation data, quality system certification, and audit points. Overall parts per million performance may be helpful for understanding where a supplier stands in relation to its competitors, but to really understand process capabilities—such as yields out of a wafer-fab, for instance—the data must be detailed enough for purchasing engineers to start working the quality problems. Although certified suppliers' processes may have reached very high performance levels that would seem to eliminate a need for detailed quality information, most customers need to continue to track and analyze parts data because of the invaluable technology information embedded in each quality report. It is important to understand yields on specific raw materials, how changes in equipment might affect production, and how to spot tooling overuse problems before they reach the customer.

What is good delivery performance? Parts where they are needed, when they are needed, and no paperwork errors. At Honda, components or systems, such as dashboard assemblies, are timed to reach the assembly lines or staging areas perfectly on time—not early, and certainly not late. Essentially, delivery performance is equated with quality standards because a missing piece is as costly as a reject, because both represent lost opportunity costs, and both require expensive replacements. At a cost of more than $20,000 per minute, line down situations are almost unheard of.

The process of data analysis, discovery, and communication builds stronger performance because it develops relationships between customers and suppliers. The work of understanding any complex production or procurement system is not completed with just the numbers; problem diagnosis and solutions extend to both sides of the fence. Responsibility to improve is not a one-sided affair but an improvement process that requires commitment and input from both sides. The key point is that there should be detailed problem-solving and permanent corrective action plans for every quality and delivery problem.

Here's another example of a relatively young company working to improve its supply management capabilities.

RESPIRONICS

When one Pennsylvania medical device producer decided to tackle some basic supply chain problems, it uncovered unexpected opportunities along the way. Respironics found that a good starting point for improving the areas of supplier quality and delivery is the supplier development project.

When Respironics looked at its supplier network, the company realized that about twenty-three companies were its key lifeline suppliers, and of those twenty-three, a few were mission critical producers that were struggling to meet their customers' high growth rates. Often entrepreneurial, innovative small- and medium-size producers are surprised with quick growth ramp-ups, and they need all the help they can get to regain control. A joint Respironics/supplier project team took the opportunity to lay out an improvement plan that followed our twelve steps. After the initial five weeks of patient process observation and data gathering, the results were stunning. Although teams may be eager to jump right in and "just do it!"—that is, move equipment, take out inventory, or build cells—we urge patience and a steady adherence to the proven methodology.

TWELVE-STEP SUPPLIER DEVELOPMENT

There are twelve steps to taking a development project from identification of the real problem to first results. This twelve-step process is essentially the path Respironics took to recraft sections of its supply chain. At certain points, the company had to stop and reevaluate, and at other times, the project moved quickly. For instance, although Respironics felt that it knew where the performance gaps were, the company really needed an extensive period of data gathering and some discussions before it was clear on the core problems. Furthermore, management may at some points need to reconvene to measure actual findings against the amount of work ahead. And finally, there is a thirteenth step to every improvement project, and that is to celebrate! Giving participants an opportunity to report results and identify next areas of opportunity, as well as celebrate an incredible achievement of fresh learning is very important, and high performers never tire of good recognition (see Figure 3–4).

Twelve Steps to Supplier Development[1]

1. Review performance gaps
2. Discuss specifics about how the project will be approached and implemented
3. Work to achieve mutual agreement on project focus
4. Identify processes that result in waste
5. Compare performance gaps with the desired state
6. Establish project metrics and metrics baselines
7. Gather and analyze data
8. Develop improvement strategies
9. Develop an implementation plan
10. Calculate the return on investment
11. Create and review a proposal with the supplier's management or ownership
12. Execute the improvement plan

Building Block #3: Technological Capabilities

Technological capabilities mean different things to different industries, but it is the responsibility of buyers to become experts

KEY STEPS TO LEAN SUPPLIERS

• Process improvement is intentional

• Investment in supplier development is specific

—Engineers assigned specifically to supplier development

Focus is on closing performance gaps

Figure 3–4. Key steps to lean suppliers.

in their current and potential new suppliers' technological capabilities. For automotive producers and their second- and third-tier suppliers, where so much work has been done in the Toyota Production System, Honda BP, and other lean methods, technological capability means the ability of a supplier to perfect its manufacturing processes—to be the low cost leader and to become completely predictable—so that the supplier offers not only the technology that its customers want now but also the capabilities they will need farther down the road. Different industries look for different types of technology advantage.

In the automotive sector, as well as many other industries, the customer is looking for reliable supplier processes, and an ability to innovate. Reliability, which is the guarantee of quality and on-time deliveries, must come first.

For the electronics sector, technological capability means something else. In high-tech companies like Flextronics whose product life cycles follow Moore's Law of shorter, faster, smaller, technological alignment, or convergence, between a customer and its suppliers is extremely important, a decision maker. Developing the knowledge of a supplier's technological capabilities, and creating alignment with new product plans, is as important as supplier development is for automotive. For high-tech companies, finding and signing up the most advanced suppliers, and identifying the new ones out there growing, is as important as fixing process problems would be for Ford, for example, in the automotive industry. A computer buyer, for instance, may tolerate slight price differences between competing products, but if the new laptop doesn't carry all the whiz-bang new options, the product is doomed. It is a waste of new product launch investments, and small price differences won't make any difference.

Building Block #4: Wavelength

Supplier responsiveness and degree of user-friendly systems and communications are important in the partnership, an indication of how well supplier management philosophies and systems align with the customer's. We call this alignment wavelength, and as a somewhat subjective standard, it indicates how well a supplier will be able to grow and flex with its customer's market requirements.

Customers and suppliers need not dress, talk, or walk alike! They don't have to look the same, and suppliers as experts in their own products and technologies are not mirror images of their customers. It is unrealistic to expect a supplier to run production, for example, exactly the same way, with the same resources and methods that a large customer would apply to a similar production challenge. Furthermore, customers are closer to market demands, because they more directly feel the impact of sudden market swings and competitive pressures, particularly in electronic or consumer goods. They may therefore require more responsiveness with less lead time than their suppliers can muster; therefore, supplier responsiveness and user-friendly systems and communications become critical to the partnership. The ability of a supplier to match its customer's pace—for example, timing hourly shipments to meet just-in-time schedules—is important in the partnership, an indication of how well supplier management philosophies and systems align with the customer's. We call this type of alignment *wavelength*. As a subjective "soft" standard, it indicates how well a supplier will be able to grow and flex up and down with its customer's market requirements.

One way for customers to begin to see the supplier's perspective, and to evaluate whether the two partners are operating on the same wavelength, is to conduct a supplier survey. In the book *Breakthrough Partnering* by Patricia E. Moody, the author offers a comprehensive partnership review in the Customer/Supplier Survey. There are three or four different versions, but the Motorola and Honda examples work universally well. A survey is important to allow close-up participants to view the business from both sides of the fence, to understand what information a supplier needs to perform well, as well as a customer's schedule and price requirements.

We recommend that customers use a neutral third-party organization to conduct the survey to guarantee the survey's integrity and to protect suppliers so that they will feel comfortable giving frank and useful opinions and data. Although the survey has proven to be valuable for companies like Motorola, Honda, IBM, and Harley-Davidson, typically most companies conduct the survey once every one or two years. It is also important to repeat the same survey, preferably with the same respondents, to track progress. Establishing a baseline is incredibly valuable when it allows customers to monitor positive (or negative) change.

Honda's purchasing department uses the survey as a partnering tool as well. Honda veterans tell the story of learning how careful the company was to present the "same face"—the same message and attitude—no matter which area of the company was speaking, such as purchasing, engineering, or production. Honda executives illustrate this concept by describing a spaghetti-like Japanese candy: When this confection is cut, the cross-sectional slice shows the outline of a smiling face, and no matter at what point on the strand the cross-section is taken, the face is always the same!

Moving from Traditional Performance to World-Class Supply Chain Levels

When companies become aware of cost problems, it's usually because they are facing layoffs and other severe cost cuts or because they need more cash to fund new products. Or perhaps, they are discovering that old standby product lines just aren't carrying the company the way they used to. The deeper the crisis, the more attention costs generate.

Although they usually look for a few easy, quick solutions, like demanding supplier price cuts, coming up with one or two more percentage points of profitability is not as easy as turning on the money machine, because every traditional cost-cutting method affects the basic corporate structure and is difficult to recover from. Why not use the power of the supply chain, and strategic sourcing to free up cash?

Seven Steps to The Incredible Payback and the Power of Strategic Sourcing

Strategic sourcing, a systematic, team-based approach to leveraging the total global spend and developing a strong supply base, creates value and intelligence to build the corporation. Strategic sourcing reinforces and strengthens the supply chain as it delivers measurable results.

Companies like John Deere discovered the power of strategic sourcing as the company moved from a traditional supply base to lean, focused operations. In less than four years, Deere changed the way the company bought materials and services, redesigned its supply network, and trimmed billions from its spend. In a largely decentralized environment, purchasing executives found innovative approaches to developing suppliers as well as overall market intelligence to carry them into bigger global operations.

Deere's strategic sourcing model includes seven steps, as shown in Figure 3–5. The company successfully applied each step, for example, to a single category of its $3 billion indirect spend for MRO. Deere had never before examined a category of buys across all plants and divisions, a centralized approach to Spend Management, and the company was eager to see the results. Executives knew that by putting just this small slice of the spend through the strategic sourcing process, the company would realize big savings, as well as uncover bad practices, and they were not disappointed. The strategic sourcing exercise conducted on just one commodity realized millions in savings. Along the way, commodity teams uncovered incredible opportunities and long-neglected practices. And the company learned a lot about its supplier partners.

First off, planners had to find out exactly how much the company was spending on MRO, when, at what price, and, most important, from whom. That meant, for the first time, central purchasing analysts tallied up Deere's total number of suppliers. The total came to 1,975 suppliers—an incredible, ragged accumu-

Step 7: Reward Winners

Step 6: Translate Progress to
Finalize and Publicize

Step 5: Verify, Track, and Control

Step 4: Meet with Suppliers

Step 3: Strategy by Commodity

Step 2: Commodity Teams

Step 1: Get the Numbers

Figure 3–5. Seven steps to strategic sourcing.

lation of big and small, long- and short-term relationships scattered across the United States. Next, in marched the MRO commodity team from purchasing, which was tasked with developing written strategies for every part. After reviewing Deere's supplier portfolio to establish criteria for selecting ongoing suppliers, team members made a second shocking discovery.

"We realized," recalls an original team member, "these were little guys who had been doing business with us a long time—some well-known old friends. Some of them even went to grammar school with senior management." Team members knew they had an awful problem on their hands. "We told our management that we had too many—1,975—suppliers, and we were paying way too much.

"We learned that although some suppliers offered Deere very good, personal service and attention, other suppliers had no electronic means of transferring information, or selling, and they were all too expensive, at least 15 to 25 percent over what should be." Clearly, it was time to reduce the number of suppliers so that planners could focus on doing a better job with fewer partners. Unfortunately, it looked like many of the 1,975 suppliers were not the kind of partners that the company needed going into its third generation.

And so, the word came back from senior management that planners should begin to trim. Buyers were instructed to go overboard on communicating the change, and when necessary, to let targeted suppliers down gently. Buyers had to give them sufficient time to formulate a winning response—or not. It was important to treat them with great respect and to keep suppliers completely informed of each step in the process.

The difficult discussions began, as planners worked their way through the suppliers' list. Team members identified the ones doing an excellent job, but curiously, none of the others really believed that Deere would ever change. The commodity team kept great records on these discussions, just in case Deere had to defend its actions.

But when it came down to the last minute of the last day and

Deere buyers started notifying suppliers that they would no longer be a supplier to Deere, "then," recalls a key team member, "they got the message. We had a few pull strings with the general manager who had kept them in business all those years. A few suppliers, when they heard 'It's out of our hands,' automatically went to the top, but it was too late—our people at the top were well informed and knew that this was part of the process of strategic sourcing."

For Deere, as well as for key suppliers, the strategic sourcing approach was a learning process as well as a financial success. *In six months, planners took the 1,975 suppliers down to 20.* As the first pass at running the entire process, the first one was slow, and it took about nine months to complete. Subsequent iterations were much quicker and completed in six months or less. A team leader warned, however, not to expect the process to take less than six months because it is important to study and know the industry, the suppliers, and other critical factors thoroughly. Commodity experts became very knowledgeable, because they are the ones who had to establish criteria for partnering with Deere. All suppliers, for instance, had to provide electronic catalogs. Surprisingly, this requirement turned out to be a significant cutoff, because 90 percent of the 1,975 could not.

By clearly defining supplier performance standards, the new partnership was more clearly mapped out. Cost Management, especially negotiation of appropriate margins—a Best Practice at which Honda excels—was very important and required a certain amount of time to do well and correctly.

Next, Deere executives sat down with suppliers to negotiate new arrangements, including margins for specific volume levels. This type of negotiation, called *open book accounting*, requires solid industry and technology knowledge going into it, because buyers need to know as much about how much it really should cost to make a specific part—labor, materials, overhead—as does the supplier. Both Honda and Toyota excel at this approach. Good negotiations guarantee the supplier a fair margin and a long-term partnership in return for good volumes and occasional help as needed in continuous improvement or new technology areas. When Deere sat down with its shortened list of suppliers, because the parts had already been deeply researched, discussions quickly moved beyond pure price issues to future partnering challenges, such as new product plans and upcoming technologies.

After Deere's purchasing people cut their teeth on their first exercise in strategic sourcing, they were ready to move on to purchases in the direct spend areas across all divisions. Because Deere was a largely decentralized organization, the central purchasing group did not dictate division results. Instead, divisional managers were urged to get together and go through the strategic sourcing work. The group was instructed to formulate the supplier performance and capabilities criteria. They were assured that they would not be forced to consolidate all castings and forgings, for example, to a single supplier. Given the choice, sometimes the division people did not consolidate the buy. With most direct materials, however, they saw the advantage of leveraging and chose to move forward with it.

Experienced Deere buyers say that their strategic sourcing process speaks to the value of increasing purchasing industry and market intelligence. Furthermore, the deeper your team's understanding of specific products, the quicker the company will move from a transactional to a more strategic mode. In-depth intelligence allows supply managers, like the ones next described at Respironics, to make strategic moves to strengthen and trim its supply base.

Restructuring the Supply Chain for Profits and Growth

Few organizations have the luxury of starting a new supply chain or production line with all the correct data and resources in place. Respironics is a good example of a healthy company interested in building a supply chain that can meet its growth rate with corresponding improvements in quality and delivery. Although the company enjoys enviable 17 percent annual growth, few viable competitors, and a growing worldwide market for innovative healthcare devices, management saw an erosion in margins caused partly by supply management problems. Respironics believed there was an opportunity, however, to generate more new products and better older ones, as well as to please Wall Street if the company could capture the full potential of its supply chain. The company felt that perhaps the supply chain held the key to higher margins and greater profitability, if it could just find the money!

We took a comprehensive look at the company's procurement strategies, including the number of suppliers they worked with, at payment terms, inventory turns, people, systems, lead times, flexibility and responsiveness, and most important, quality and technology capabilities. We found big and small opportunities throughout the enterprise and so many pockets of advantage that the first challenge was deciding where to start.

We also evaluated the company's strengths and weaknesses to understand how easy it might be to begin making changes. Respironics people are fearless innovators who seize new ideas, like lean manufacturing's single piece flow, and adapt them to their own internal conditions. With almost no outside help, Respironics's engineers are happy to track down a new methodology, perhaps with the help of a book or a benchmarking visit, to learn the new process. They are quick studies, and in an area filled with complexity and obvious risks, their entrepreneurial spirit carries them far. On the other side of the balance sheet, we found that Respironics had too many things on their plate, too much to do in the midst of a healthy growth spurt. They needed help to sharpen their focus on the few critical, achievable tasks that would immediately improve the supply chain.

The company decided to launch a strategic sourcing initiative with three new purchasing professionals—two to work on supplier development and one to do Cost Management—to free up millions in hidden dollars. In year one, supplier consolidation and performance monitoring yielded three times their additional investment in two supplier development engineers. By year two, the gains were increasing, and by year's end, savings tallied up to a whopping four times the original investment. Projections for the next phase of the strategic sourcing initiative remained strong as twenty-three key suppliers were scheduled to collaborate with their high-growth customer.

Respironics and its partner suppliers took a hard look at financials before it was too late. Other older organizations might take longer to achieve The Incredible Paybacks they deserve, but we know that even somewhat arthritic and inflexible operations can realize substantial initial benefits from a few starter projects. MRO, for instance, is an area that always offers huge returns.

Consider a Signing Bonus

One unique approach that delivers savings as it cements strong relationships is the signing bonus. According to Chicago-based supply management consultant Jim Bergman, this approach eliminates sales and marketing work as it delivers savings that go directly to the bottom line; it should be used occasionally, however, as circumstances dictate, and should not become a standard mode of operation.

Here's how a signing bonus works. Giant Inc. is looking for high quality, perfect delivery and great prices from its plastics suppliers. Giant is currently paying five suppliers from $60 to $80 per plastic injected molded unit. Jones Inc., another new plastics molder, comes in with a quote of $70, and better quality, plus they will help with design. Jones offers Giant a 2 percent signing bonus to seal the deal and build relationship, prove value to shareholders, and grow Jones's business. Sometimes a signing bonus is extended to offset Bill of Material prices; the bonus may be paid out, for instance, during the first twelve months of the resulting contract, thereby allowing the customer to show stakeholders immediate value.

Start with the Seven Steps

The seven basic steps to strategic sourcing begin to capture Incredible Paybacks, but if an organization can achieve only the first two or three, it will find the momentum gained from picking low-hanging fruit may well carry the company into more difficult areas.

At Respironics, steps #1 through #4 were immediately tackled by supply management. Work on the remaining steps was planned for future projects, because they knew that these would take longer than the initial steps.

STEP 1: STUDY THE NUMBERS

To set preliminary payback goals, first identify the total purchasing spend: all monies spent on indirect and direct materials, and other company expenses such as supplier development, training, travel, benefits, outsourced or purchased materials. Any and all expenditures are subject to review; traditionally many companies only consider materials used in production, tooling, or repair or maintenance materials, but "soft" expenditures like temporary personnel contracts and healthcare insurance plans can be just as important.

Most companies will find it difficult to produce a total spend figure that tracks with spend groups. Deere filled this gap with a college intern who was able to accumulate actual steel invoices from around the world to calculate the company's global steel spend. It is important to start with the rolled-up total, as well as detailed expenditures. Although it may take some time, one method for assembling the numbers is from paid invoices, or from actual supplier records.

Next, set a macro-percentage goal of savings per year, per quarter. It is important to pick a percentage target that is achievable: If you set the bar too high, management will be disappointed with initial results; if you set the bar too low, no one will truly discover the depth of opportunities. We generally recommend that purchasers think about their level of maturity and their supplier capabilities before they pick a percentage target.

Any and every company can achieve savings of 2 to 3 percent of total spend by simple attention to the basics. Sustained savings of 5 percent or more require organizational change and new policies, while savings above 5 percent year after year require expert strategic sourcing prowess. Five percent savings are difficult, but not impossible, to achieve year after year.

It will help to identify common parts and commodities across plants and divisions because these items will offer great opportunity for leverage and consolidation. Be sure to prioritize opportunities, however, by which ones are most likely to yield the percentage savings target you are looking for.

STEP 2: FORM COMMODITY TEAMS TO ATTACK OPPORTUNITY AREAS BY AREA, COMMODITY, OR SUPPLIER GROUP

The teams should cover distinct technology or product groups, like printed circuit boards or metal stampings. Because the teams develop in-depth supplier and market/technology intelligence, they are the contributors that are most capable of helping to prioritize opportunity areas. Commodity teams ideally should be cross-functional because total product cost is created by several different areas in the supply chain—engineering and manufacturing, for example, as well as purchasing.

If your company has a separate new product introduction group, it needs to be represented on the team as well. Chrysler, IBM, and Motorola are great models of procurement innovators who rely on commodity teams. More than ten years ago, Chrysler platform teams pioneered this cross-functional collaborative approach that brought technical expertise into life cycle planning and preparation. If engineering is not active on the commodity team, results will be limited and hard to sustain, because over 90 percent of the cost of most products is determined in early development stages. Likewise, when manufacturing is not adequately represented, the team will miss opportunities to pick the right suppliers with the best processes. Manufacturing's contribution to team savings and launch dates is equally valuable; production should take an active role to standardize parts, one solid approach to savings.

The role of commodity teams is to gather technology, manufacturing, and market intelligence, along with purchasing information, so that a complete picture and a written strategy can be developed for every commodity and every critical part. This is especially important when companies decide to reduce the supply base and active part numbers.

Finally, because the commodity team is also involved in supplier selection and development, it is important for team members to have access to plenty of help doing lean methods, including kaizen mapping, 3P (Product and Process Preparation, a Toyota development approach) for new product development, and supplier surveys.[2]

We recommend visiting experienced plant sites, benchmarking, and participating on other teams to learn the methods. When the team is familiar with relative cost savings from various methods, it will have a better shot at hitting cost targets.

STEP 3: EVALUATE NEEDS AND DEVELOP A STRATEGY FOR EACH COMMODITY

Every commodity has different technology and pricing strategies, and it's important to rank the commodities by degree of difficulty. The team can then identify first-pass targets for spend improvements by starting with the low-hanging fruit, such as MRO, air and hotel expenses, or raw materials, to build enthusiasm for the new approach and to develop experience on the team. The more-challenging commodities will be easier because immediate and impressive gains build momentum, hope, and enthusiasm for the harder tasks to come.

In a decentralized organization, this is the point at which the sourcing strategy, by group, needs to be communicated to business unit or product managers.

Furthermore, although most information systems will capture reasonably up-to-date product cost data, for key components or parts groups, the commodity team may need to develop total cost of ownership data to evaluate true costs. If a part, for instance, requires significant maintenance, these costs needed to be added to the initial purchase price.

Total Cost of Ownership = A + (O + T + M + W + R + E) less S,

Where—

A = Acquisition cost

O = Operating costs (includes transportation, customs and duties)

T = Training costs

M = Maintenance costs

W = Warehousing costs (including inventory in the entire supply chain)

R = Risks (including things like currency exchange–rate risk)

E = Environmental costs

S = Salvage value

STEP 4: MEET WITH KEY SUPPLIERS TO REVIEW TOTAL COST OBJECTIVES, INDIVIDUAL PRODUCT COSTS, QUALITY PERFORMANCE, DEVELOPMENT GAPS, AND RECOVERY PLANS

Your supply management metrics should include good cost breakdowns by part and commodity group, as well as quality performance history and notes on special issues. Furthermore, technology and market information outlining forecasted trends and competitive issues from both suppliers and the customer will help frame discussions along strategic lines. For many suppliers, this will be the first time they have pulled together this type of meeting, first with high-level executives, followed by operating personnel.

Good data becomes even more important as a framework for data-driven reviews.

For many suppliers, their first operating challenge is to become lean by adopting basic Toyota or Honda production systems methods. Before undertaking serious lean initiatives, however, it is important to evaluate how far along a production facility is, and that job falls to the purchasing engineers. On a typical walk-through, they will be looking for cleanup and organizing opportunities as well as other improvement targets. In Honda BP, this may begin with COPDS—clean up, organize, pick up, discipline, and safety. An operation that has not tackled these simple lean improvements will have many opportunities that translate to inventory and productivity gains and better flows. An area that has already begun kaizen work, or has redesigned flows and installed cellular one-piece flow and significantly improved inventory turns, will look for savings in harder-to-reach areas.

Step Five: Verify, Track, and Control

This step in strategic sourcing needs great emphasis because it is frequently misunderstood and neglected. Many supply management groups develop tremendous savings opportunities, but somehow they do not retain significant profit impact because the savings are not tracked and controlled. That is why it is very important as savings appear to Verify, Track, and Control (VTC) every item.

In Chapter 6, Metrics for The Incredible Payback, we emphasize the importance of having the finance department verify savings gleaned from improvement programs, and tracking the permanent reduction of budgets to reinforce continued savings. Without a disciplined and routine VTC procedure for monitoring spend savings, the money will simply disappear and have little or no impact on bottom-line profits.

For example, one Midwestern auto equipment producer used strategic sourcing to reduce travel expenses. Purchases were consolidated with one partner/supplier; purchasing also negotiated hotel and rental car discounts that helped contribute to millions of dollars in savings. But executives could not understand how, after more than a year of clear improvement in travel costs, overall budgeted expenditures continued to rise. The savings seemed to have evaporated! Where was the money going, and who was responsible? Unfortunately, the answer proved to be all so understandable and quite human. Although the strategic sourcing process cut travel expenditures by over 15 percent, mostly due to intelligent consolidation to single sources, department managers did not reduce their next year travel budgets. Instead, the hundreds of thousands of dollars saved simply went into more trips, more domestic and overseas travel, and more hotel stays! Yes, the savings could be verified and the ongoing costs could be tracked, but the third part of a VTC routine—which is Control—was completely missing from the department manager's process. Hard-earned savings quickly disappeared into new and creative expenditures.

Step 6: Translate Supply Management Gains to Positive Changes in the Income Statement, and Publicize

Good news travels fast if it's made public. If the Midwestern auto supplier that realized hundreds of thousands in savings had produced revised lower budgets and rolled-up expenses to a reduced cost of goods sold (COGS) line item in the income statement, which would have incidentally increased profits, annual savings would have been sustained and repeated. That is why it is necessary to tie projected and actual savings directly into the top-level income statement. These financials are management's control system, and when chief financial and operations executives understand the source of COGS savings from supply management strategic initiatives, they will be able to plan for the gains. Furthermore, when the news of increased profits makes its way to shareholders and auditors, everyone's enthusiasm for supply chain change builds.

The contributions of chief procurement officers to profitability, when recognized and understood by shareholders, enable The Incredible Payback. Furthermore, profitable supply chain operations drive better compensation packages. Ten years ago, there was only a handful of millionaire purchasing executives. Today, the number has multiplied, and there is no limit to the work and the rewards that lie ahead.

A well-publicized comparison of previous costs against project results and future stated targets should also be included in management review of strategic sourcing progress.

STEP 7: REVISIT SUPPLY CHAIN PARTNERS AND RELEASE NONPERFORMERS; RECOGNIZE AND REWARD WINNERS

Many good initiatives—whether they are kaizen or strategic sourcing—fizzle after the first ground-breaking results. That is the reason we urge procurement to continually revisit supply chain performance data and to maintain high standards by eliminating bad performance. That does not mean that when the supply base has been trimmed, as we mentioned in the John Deere safety equipment commodity group, that the remaining twenty suppliers must be cut to a handful. Instead, we urge buyers to examine their options: Supplier development, training, and joint study projects are a few of the many positive opportunities to improvement. Elimination of strategic suppliers is a last resort that most companies cannot afford to do, even in a healthy economy.

Honda and Deere supplier performance recognition days are well-recognized and appreciated in North American industry. Every April, Honda invites more than three hundred suppliers to an awards and recognition Supplier Day. It's a well-orchestrated event filled with music, good food, awards and applause for the high-performing winners, photos, and an unusual opportunity to meet and rate the competition.

Honda takes the opportunity at that gathering to talk about new product strategic planning, and to share corporate and technology trends. Respironics held its first annual supplier celebration day after the beginnings of its strategic sourcing project, and suppliers were eager to hear more. It was important for suppliers to understand where Respironics saw its business going, where the high-growth opportunities wait, and its plans to get there. Management's expectation that savings would have a direct impact on Respironics's income statement was reinforced when supplier team members discovered how to take 20 percent out of the cost of one of their main respiration products.

Finally, one success opens possibilities for more. When team members learned first-hand how to apply their new productivity tools to problems, they wanted to do more. And when Respironics's buyers saw how well and quickly results could be achieved with just one supplier project, they were anxious to help others.

Let's look at how a technology giant, Lucent Technologies, handles its global supply chain challenges. Lucent has a great deal of experience with product introductions, and the company's supply chain deserves considerable credit for its repeated successful launches. Lucent is working in an advanced payback area that includes the best technology leaders.

How Lucent Designs Costs Out of Its Supply Chain

More than 90 percent of the cost of any new product is determined at the early design stages, when decisions about materials, specifications, manufacturing processing, and even packaging are made. This area of new product development holds many opportunities for big paybacks, but not all operations are ready to tackle design issues at the level that will influence component design and selection. A few companies, including Lucent Technologies, are working hard through supply chain management and engineering to take costs out early, before they accumulate.

Jose Mejia, president of Lucent's supply chain network, confirms that his group does more than direct product designers to preferred suppliers.

Lucent Payback

Lucent buyers look at supplier reuse and other issues such as standardization and postponement that cover the design of the supply chain itself. Mejia believes that Lucent's supply chain innovation is paying off with better product margins resulting from more cost-efficient product design, smoother processes, and a comprehensive, integrated approach to quality.

Mejia instructs Lucent's buyers to ask the following ten questions during the design stage because the answers will take Lucent supply chain people into a higher performance level and more new challenges:

Ten Questions Lucent Buyers Ask During Design[3]

1. Who are the customers for the new product?
2. Where in the world are the customers located?
3. What is the target cost for the new product?
4. How will target cost change over time?
5. What is the percentage of component reuse in the new product?
6. What is the percentage of weight or space taken out of the new product compared with previous products?
7. What are the quality and reliability requirements of the new product?
8. What percent of the Bill of Material (B.O.M.) will come from strategic suppliers?
9. What is the level of customization in the B.O.M.?
10. What percent of the B.O.M. is standard components?

"I do not believe that companies actually get the full value they could from their supply chains if they do not engage with the designers in the early stages of developing the product and working toward standardization and alignment on what the company is trying to do the for the market and the customer." Mejia cites Lucent wireless and mobility product groups in which the design of its products was developed using the a limited number of technology platforms. Standardizing on a few platforms allows reuse of a significant proportion of design in new products, and saves money and time.

For switching products and optical products, Lucent actually has its manufacturing partners participate in the design phase, making it easier for the engineers to incorporate what is readily available in product. Mejia is proud of the significant progress his group is making in reducing costs well before they accumulate, "It's paying off in inventory reduction and margin improvements—across the board. In less than three years, we went from 1.4 turns of inventory to 7.8, and Lucent's gross margins increased by some 25 percentage points. While there likely will be variations from quarter to quarter, those results clearly include the sustainable impact of our operational improvements and cost reductions. Delivery performance, which we have measured since the company has been in business, started at less than 70 percent, but now we are in the 90 percent range." Mejia believes that number reflects the company's growing responsiveness in a marketplace that is under tremendous pressure. He notes that sometimes "we don't know until the last minute exactly what they want, so we had to create an exceptionally flexible and robust supply chain."

Preparing the supply chain means designing for postponement, a build strategy that Hewlett Packard pioneered, as well as standardization and parts reuse. Postponement means that a product is designed to be built as a standard unit, and only "customerized" at the very end of the production cycle. For example, if designers want to offer a different keyboard for Greek, Russian, or Chinese alphabets, they can customize in two ways. The first approach builds the Greek keyboard into the unit at the beginning of production. Therefore, planners must forecast and stock what they hope will be the right number of keyboards headed to Greece. If they guess wrong, either excess inventories or expensive expedites occur. But if the computer is designed to specify Greek or Russian or Chinese key tabs at the end of the cycle, just before the unit is wrapped in foam and shipped off the dock, postponement saves lead time, expedites, and excess inventories. The same approach is being used by Nokia to streamline its cell phone supply chains. When designers use the same internal chips wherever possible, for instance, they make customers happy, and they take out costly supply chain complexity.

Mejia cites one more Lucent supply chain success story: From the signing of the agreement to flipping the switch, the installation of a wireless infrastructure for an Asian region took only sixty days, enabling the customer to begin generating revenue much sooner than would have been possible under a normal deployment schedule.

Unfortunately, Mejia believes that in 95 percent of our companies, the criticality of the supply chain is not fully understood. "It's not just about manufacturing and purchasing. Purchasing is often dispersed to many different business units, and that means no one is thinking strategically, and they certainly are not designing the process to take advantage of market opportunities and make money. You can have the best product design, but if the supply chain doesn't get it there, that's not good enough. If you need too much inventory, if you don't improve the cost structure, you are severely hampering your ability to profitably meet the needs of your customers."

Mejia is concerned about a supply chain organization's ability to be competitive globally. "When you are competing on a global basis, there will be some intense dynamics in places where you have to compete on a different kind of playing field. For instance, too often when North American companies make decisions about manufacturing in China, it's all about labor costs, but the government of China is extremely connected with their businesses. The question becomes, how do you compete with that when the U.S. government takes a different approach to business? It's going to be a big problem for business in this country; a big supply chain problem from all perspectives—resources, economy. It started with low-end materials, and now it involves manufacturing and technology and high-level software, so we have to compete in a game that has changed dramatically. We're forced to do things ten times different and faster and better to win. Lucent has done well in India, and in China we have the largest market share of the wireless infrastructure, so we are winning in some of the countries that are supposed to be lowest cost. But that's because we went to China and established ourselves there. For example, we have a Bell Labs facility there. Our manufacturing partner has a facility there, so we are playing in that market as a local participant, not as someone from the outside."

Conclusion

In this chapter, we looked at companies that have built high-performing supply chains, and one company that has begun the process, and how they did it. Each operation starts with the same basics—Cost Management, a report card on supplier quality and delivery, an evaluation of suppliers' technological capabilities, and wavelength—and moves on from there.

We've shown the payback numbers and the three levels of payback capabilities from beginners to expert. Strategic sourcing, as detailed by John Deere, is one of the disciplines that will take supply chains into big paybacks, year after year.

When executives look at the power of supply chain managers to return hard cash to the income statement, they want proof. Shareholders and analysts, as well, need to see the results in real numbers, and strategic sourcing delivers the kind of payback everyone needs. Strategic sourcing as a discipline organizes and prioritizes all the disparate actions and agendas that occupy enterprise leaders. When commodity team members, for instance, find good ways to collaborate internally with manufacturing and engineering, profits rise. When suppliers offer their hard-won expertise to help launch better products, everyone benefits.

We offer a few clear, high-value approaches to Incredible Paybacks. If your operation understands lean methods but wants to sustain double-digit savings, keep going and think bigger and harder about harnessing the intelligence of strategic sourcing. If your company, like so many out there, is having trouble keeping up with global competitors, and you are looking for a high-level, clear, and measurable approach, remember Lucent's ten questions.

The Best Practice experts start with good data and work with suppliers to improve every key performance number. Payback in some commodities is immediate; others take longer and require some investment to upgrade the organization. We believe, however, that every minute spent on data gathering and analysis strengthens supply management's position and builds management support for your next move.

Notes

1. R. Dave Nelson, "Manufacturing Solutions," *Automotive Engineering International*, August 1999, p. 68, as reprinted in *The Purchasing Machine*, by Dave Nelson, Patricia E. Moody, and Jonathan Stegner (New York: The Free Press, 2001), p. 138. (For further insight into mapping, see *Learning to See*, by James Womack and John Shook (Brookline, Mass.: Lean Enterprise Institute, 1999).

2. For detailed information on how to conduct kaizen projects, see Anthony C. Laraia, Patricia E. Moody, and Robert W. Hall, *The Kaizen Blitz* (New York: John Wiley & Sons, 1999). For supply chain mapping, see *Learning to See*, by James Womack and John Shook (Brookline, Mass.: Lean Enterprise Institute, 1999). For 2P/3P New Product/Process Preparation, see Anand Sharma and Patricia E. Moody, *The Perfect Engine* (New York: The Free Press). For supplier surveys, see Patricia E. Moody, *Breakthrough Partnering* (New York: John Wiley & Sons, 1993).

3. Jose Mejia, Lucent Technologies, 2003.

Chapter 4

Working with Suppliers

"What's the point of working with suppliers to help them improve their processes? They're big kids, why can't they do it themselves? And when they get better, won't they be helping my competition by offering lower prices and shorter lead times? Where's the payback in that? Maybe they will give away our secrets!"

Well, yes and no. For example, when Honda in the early 1990s started to receive recognition for its unique purchasing practices, many observers, especially automotive competitors, were eager to understand exactly what was happening down there in Marysville, Ohio. Honda's benchmarking exchanges and seminars were open to all takers, even those from competitors like Ford and Chrysler. However, GM trekkers were soon met with reluctance as Honda executives learned that the exchange was one-sided, and that their buyers were not allowed open access to GM. An opportunity to raise the bar and use competition to elicit even higher levels of performance in the supply chain was somehow passed by.

Still, the impact of Honda's development work with suppliers continued to have a big impact on the auto industry as a whole.

The good news spread, and within five years of the Marysville complex start-up, dozens of local suppliers had achieved perfect levels of quality and delivery performance. They had set up good processes, learned trouble-shooting and data-review techniques, and were well positioned to continue on their own to reach degrees of excellence never seen before in the auto industry. What had been an area of "de-industrialization" at the edge of the rust belt began to blossom with new growth and great potential. The new suppliers made history for their customers. Just as North American companies have rushed to learn Six Sigma and lean methods, so has supplier development, the practice of helping suppliers develop their capabilities, made sense. The payback appeared early and grew, and the numbers continue to support the advantages of supplier development.

Dr. Robert Handfield, director of the Supply Chain Resource Consortium at North Carolina State University, looked at the types of supplier development being conducted by major automotive producers and their payback. He found that supplier development strategies can result in significant improvements in supplier performance, including:

❑ Reducing product defects by 5 to 90 percent
❑ Improving on-time delivery by 6 to 15 percent
❑ Reducing order fulfillment cycle time by 30 to 80 percent
❑ Improving product performance by 10 to 30 percent[1]

Handfield concluded, however, that not all supplier development initiatives are successful—as many as 50 percent are not because of poor implementation and follow-up. He classified supplier development approaches into four types: the rewarding method ("The Carrot"), penalizing poor performance ("The Stick"), ongoing detailed assessment and feedback ("Measurement"), and direct involvement in suppliers' operations ("Hands-On"). Handfield's team looked at which supplier development approaches are the most effective, and concluded that a combination may be best, depending on the circumstances, the nature of the supplier, the commodity type, and the management team at the supplier.

Honda BP, Kaizen Blitz, and Lean Paybacks

After fifteen years, the Honda BP program, a cousin of the Toyota Production System, had reached 90 companies with over 120 projects touching more than 120,000 employees in North America alone. The biggest gains were in productivity and quality; cost-down averaged a conservatively reported 7.25 percent, with many cost reductions well above that number.

Productivity overall (total pieces per hour measured before and after BP) increased	47 percent
Quality improvement overall	30 percent

Several Honda suppliers racked up early, impressive gains as they tackled improvement projects on the floor and in the office. The BP projects covered a range of industries, from stampings—one of the first candidates for improvement—to plastics and electronics. Parker Hannifin, an early Honda BP adopter, spent $15,000 for twenty-five projects that saved $107,000 each on average, for a payback multiplier of 7. Other traditional kaizen metrics showed equally impressive results:

WIP ($)	98 percent reduction
Cycle time	89 percent
Distance moved	81 percent
Productivity (pieces per hour)	46 percent increase

At one Honda component plant in Mexico, hard-working teams who assembled and tested Accord master power-window switches achieved historic results on twenty-three lines spread through four departments:

Operator headcount (workers redeployed)	25.24 percent reduction per project
Suggestion system	10 ideas per associate
Average daily production rate	15.24 percent increase per project
Cycle time reduction	19.19 percent per project
Average waste cost reduction	82.11 percent per project
Average downtime reduction	54.15 percent per project

Learning and Growing the Process

As Honda and its suppliers continued to attack waste and inefficiencies, as well as quality issues, they developed a sense of what to expect after completing the initial walkthrough and data gathering. High-quality rejects, for example, meant a process was not in control, while excess inventory scattered throughout an operation meant that the entire workflow needed to be reviewed. However, a few problems tended to show up repeatedly among small- and medium-size suppliers: quality issues around scrap and rejects, and scheduling concerns. Other issues may show up periodically, but quality and delivery remain king. Quality and delivery problems are usually solvable within a few weeks or less, as Honda supplier engineers proved repeatedly with their thirteen-week BP work, and the payback is immediate.

Time Frame for Paybacks

The time frame for change under Honda BP and other kaizen approaches is short: thirteen weeks for Honda and less for the

Kaizen Blitz. Even practitioners new to lean methods can expect to see encouraging results on their first projects. Most kaizen projects—whether they are called Honda BP, Kaizen Blitz, the Toyota Production System, or simply lean methods—have an immediate impact that multiplies productivity two, three, four, or more times. The Association for Manufacturing Excellence's book on its Kaizen Blitz recorded the following improvements among dozens of companies in a range of industries, from healthcare to tool making and electronics:[2]

Setup time reduction	70 – 90 percent
Productivity improvement	20 – 60 percent
Process time reduction	40 – 80 percent
Inventory reduction	30 – 70 percent
Walking distance reduction	40 – 90 percent

Where to Begin?

By the time the new approach to cell design and quality methods reached beyond the first kaizen conducted at automotive and aerospace facilities, customers and suppliers were ready to seek bigger paybacks. Their hope was to extend individual successes to the entire enterprise, and to synchronize flows so that material movement along complex material networks became transparent and nearly seamless. They discovered that by mapping material flows, work processes, inventory positions, and other critical information in a single document, they could more deliberately identify and select targets for improvement. It was not possible for early adopters to focus on all key suppliers simultaneously, but working with a handful always justified the cost of development engineers.

As more companies learned lean methods, a few expert implementers emerged, among them Delphi Corporation, the award-winning GM spin-off. Delphi has experienced the full range of lean production history, from pioneering efforts in shop floor kaizen to full-blown enterprise-wise change and massive supply management changes. Now, Delphi continues its own lean journey, as a second-generation pioneer, while it continues to help its suppliers implement lean methods.

The Delphi Experience: Twenty-Time Shingo Prize Winner

The Delphi experience runs the gamut of lean history, from working with Japanese *sensei*, in order to absorb the Toyota process, to mapping supplier processes to launch them on their own improvement journeys. The company has grown from a captive automotive supplier reporting to GM Detroit to an innovation machine, producing patents and new technologies and bringing them to market.

But Delphi is a supply chain and manufacturing process innovator as well. In the early 1990s, the company became serious about lean methods; and by 2004, Delphi plants had won twenty Shingo Prizes. This includes sites from Flint, Michigan; Warren, Ohio; and Kokono, Indiana to the Baja coast and Mexico City, Mexico.

Delphi's work in lean methods had its official foundation in synchronous manufacturing and the Quality Network, a joint process with the United Auto Workers and International Union of Electrical Workers in the United States. This led to the creation of the Delphi Manufacturing System (DMS) and the Delphi Engineering System. According to Doug Hathaway, Delphi's manager of supplier development, who reports to the director of purchasing lean operations, the company's lean focus is contagious. Hathaway's job is to move lean into the supply base, to create the common process and organizational structure to make that happen, to staff it, and to execute.

According to Hathaway, Delphi has forty supplier development engineers in the field around the world, developing European, Asia Pacific, and North American sites. He traces the roots of the DMS to the mid-1990s when a group of Delphi professionals, mostly engineers from various divisions, were sent to benchmark the best and bring their experiences back. They were directed to create a system that kept the foundation of the Quality Network and would work throughout Delphi worldwide. Delphi's customers at Toyota, Honda, and Suzuki were very helpful. These relationships, coupled with the GM partnership at NUMMI provided valuable input to the details of DMS.

Delphi continues to accelerate its rate of lean adoptions, but there have been bumps in the road. By August 2002, when Hathaway came on board in Global Supply Management, although there were seven people in supplier development, the company lacked an integrated process and was not executing in the field. "We had pockets of some training, the right ideas, but we weren't doing it fast enough, and we weren't training suppliers to use a value-stream map or sharing successful implementation processes that were working with Delphi. A value stream map is wallpaper unless you know how to use it to execute change," warns Hathaway. Delphi suppliers needed more: They were key to the company achieving the levels of performance that Hathaway knew were possible.

The Glass Wall

Hathaway recalls experiencing a sense of frustration when he realized that Delphi could be doing much more that it was doing: "So we recognized that we were, in many cases, just giving them charts to put up on walls. Now, we've made our process more action-oriented. We have changed the process and we are using what we call The Glass Wall, a system where you use value stream mapping to drive improvement, based on metrics."

Implementation grew to include twenty-six outside suppliers by the spring of 2003, covering three commodities: electrical, metals, and chemical. Other commodities touched by the Delphi System include stamping, molding, circuit boards, and tubing components for power steering. Two-person teams work the projects in which Phase One generally lasts about ninety days. "In [those] ninety days," says Hathaway, "we use value stream mapping to identify waste and then we use the lean tools to eliminate it and provide significant, double-digit metrics improvements." Delphi worked closely with Jim Womack, the Lean Enterprise Institute founder and author of *Lean Thinking* and John Shook, coauthor of *Learning to See*. The results were measurable and showed considerable improvement.

Although many kaizen processes have been initiated without first conducting a value stream map that takes a comprehensive look at the whole process, we recommend not proceeding without one. Figure 4–1 shows an example of this approach.

In this example of value stream mapping, the Current State shows a process directed by production control; material moves through the process step-by-step, with wait times identified at some points in the operation. The current state metrics show that the process has quality problems (first-time quality stands at 5,000) as well as productivity challenges (operational availability 60 percent). After mapping, data gathering, and review, the Delphi team was able to identify different material and information flows that reduced defects, scrap, floor space, wait time, and travel distance for the parts. Furthermore, information flows were geared toward meeting real demand requirements.

Finally, team members drew up a list of several critical action items to implement the change from the current to the future flow process, including developing a changeover plan to move to cellular manufacturing and implement pull.

Delphi believes in working the plan and publicizing project results. Project metrics, which are instantly posted on Delphi's Web-based system, include the following payback success stories:

Map the Current State

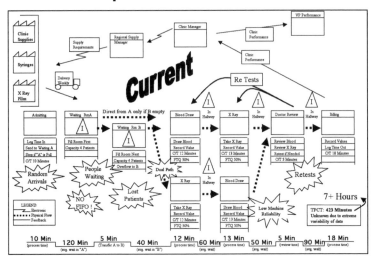

Analyze the Current State
and Design the Future State

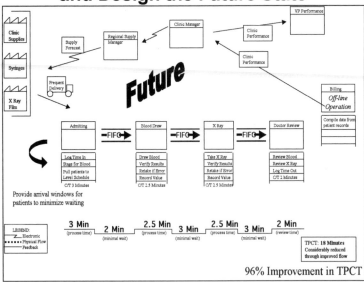

Figure 4–1. Value stream mapping process.

Develop Action Plan
Responsibility & Tie to Metrics Improvement

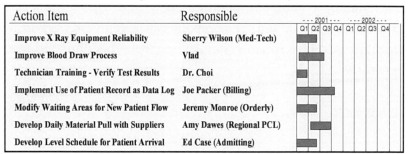

Action Item	Responsible
Improve X Ray Equipment Reliability	Sherry Wilson (Med-Tech)
Improve Blood Draw Process	Vlad
Technician Training - Verify Test Results	Dr. Choi
Implement Use of Patient Record as Data Log	Joe Packer (Billing)
Modify Waiting Areas for New Patient Flow	Jeremy Monroe (Orderly)
Develop Daily Material Pull with Suppliers	Amy Dawes (Regional PCL)
Develop Level Schedule for Patient Arrival	Ed Case (Admitting)

Metrics

Plan Targets	Current	Image	% Improve
Operators Per Shift	12	6	50%
PPHR	30	45	50%
First Time Quality	5,000	3,000	40%
Operational Availability	60	90	50%
Scrap (%)	9	3	66%
Floor Space (Sq. Ft.)	10,000	7,000	30%
TPCT	16	4	75%

Figure 4-1. Value stream mapping process (*cont.*).

Example #1:

For a Midwestern American company producing steel stampings and assemblies for the automotive industry:

60 percent improvement in productivity
55 percent improvement in lead time
60 percent reduction of scrap
first-time quality increased 33 percent
operational availability (uptime) 25 percent

The Delphi team utilized many key concepts. Two of the concepts, cells and continuous flow, were used in specific areas as appropriate. By creating a smoother flow and setting up cells, productivity soared, and the company was able to cut back from two shifts to one. Kanban systems and level scheduling reduced inventories.

Example #2:

In the northeastern United States, at an injection-molding and assembly facility that makes heating, ventilation, and air-conditioning ductwork for automotive producers, Delphi supplier development team members racked up these results after one Delphi Manufacturing System project:

Productivity improvement was 57 percent
Uptime (Operational Availability) increased 25 percent
Inventory dropped 43 percent
Scrap was cut 60 percent
Floor space was cut 27 percent

"Inspect What You Expect . . ."

"Now," says Hathaway, "because we are working with suppliers to build long-term relationships, if they can build more product at a lower cost, it's good. Here's another interesting metric—we track part travel distance sometimes, from the time it starts out until the end, and we reduced travel distance by 87 percent, from 2000 feet to 260 feet." Hathaway credits the value stream map his team drew with producing these results. "We go back and help them with the others—it is the model that they can use for improving the rest of the plant."

That's not the end of the Delphi development team, however. "After the first project, we continue to work with them, and we'll come back to them in a cadence that is appropriate to their needs. We want to teach them the project after we implement. Delphi's template for change says that supplier development people can probably expect to be in there a couple days every two weeks to answer questions, guide workshops, and audit as if you were the leader. One of the things we say," continues Hathaway, "is 'You have to inspect what you expect, or don't you don't get it.'"

Pick Your Battles

Although lean manufacturing ideally calls for the review of all processes in all production areas, few companies have the resources or the enthusiasm to conduct multiple, simultaneous improvement projects throughout their supply base. For beginners, it takes money and time, but more important, companies must maintain an intense focus and high energy levels in the midst of current production demands.

Furthermore, when production schedule requirements seem to conflict with kaizen objectives, teams need the highest level management support and attention to maintain that momentum for change. By focusing on low-hanging fruit for initial kaizen efforts, or by tackling high scrap processes, as so many projects do, companies realize better paybacks on limited improvement resources.

Starting with the Optimal Network Design

There is one additional mapping exercise that we recommend wherever possible, and that is enterprise mapping, and network optimization using smart software. It's a more advanced approach for completing lean implementation, target identification, and smoothing network flows that involves network design *first*, to minimize bottlenecks, improve throughput, and reduce inventory waste. Good logistics providers and distribution experts offer optimization software capable of evaluating all variables and parameters, and recommending the best material flows. It's a simple matter of specifying exactly what limits need to be built into the network. Are component materials required every four hours, for instance, and is there a specific sequence to deliveries? Or, what would it cost to schedule premium transport for the top twelve critical assemblies?

Good optimization software can answer all these questions and more, and produce endless simulation scenarios that balance parameters to find a best case, then lay out projected paybacks and spend.

We believe that experienced lean practitioners should review their entire network of material flows and material processing *before* they attempt massive culture change. Although most distribution and logistics networks cannot be designed from scratch, they can always be optimized and evaluated for their impact on the total spend. The software will always find paybacks in complex systems—it's simply a matter of running the simulation with the right parameters. Logistics.com, for example, a new software provider now affiliated with Manhattan Associates, is a good place to look at software optimization capabilities to supplement lean methods.

Finding The Incredible Payback in a Complex Logistics Network

Like procurement, logistics, and distribution, the material movement piece of the supply chain contributes enormous value to the supply chain; logistics and distribution are big-ticket items that have undergone rapid changes in the past ten years. Technology tools, like optimization software and quality methods, have moved the best logistics providers miles ahead of their competition. Any supply base that includes suppliers, depots, warehouses, distribution centers, or even just trucks on the road, holds the potential for big financial paybacks as well as enormous service improvement by optimizing their networks.

Schneider National, Inc., North America's largest privately held truckload carrier and one of the world's best transport and logistics providers, opened the doors of its current headquarters in Green Bay, Wisconsin, back in 1935 when Al "A.J." Schneider sold the family car to purchase his first truck. He put Schneider on the map—and on the move—and today, Schneider is not only big, but it's a source of supply chain innovation and return on investment as well. In fact, *Information Week* ranked Schneider number sixty-seven in the year 2000 for transforming core business models to ones that are dependent on IT and Internet technologies.

In 1993, the company launched a wholly owned subsidiary, Schneider Logistics, to help customers with freight management issues in their complex supply chains. Drawing on people, process, and technology, Schneider found it could create value solutions for big and small shippers, suppliers, and carriers alike.

Schneider continues to bring new products to market, including Schneider Convergence Network™, a service that provides inventory planning and control with precision never before seen. We've tracked the growth of Schneider's expertise and offerings from its first involvement with Honda, Marysville, on through Deere's task of creating a winning logistics and supply chain strategy. Both Deere and Honda supply chain executives were aware of the increasing complexity of their supply chains, and they felt that they needed to benchmark the industry, look at the important issues facing the industry, and develop a comprehensive strategy that would take them into the next generation of material movement. They knew there was money (and time) to be pulled out of the supply chain, but they needed expert help to do it.

Two eager managers made the trip up to Green Bay and met with current chairman, then CEO, Don Schneider, son of the founder. Later discussions included Chris Lofgren, former vice president of Engineering and Systems of Schneider Logistics,

Schneider National's current president and CEO. What they saw in Green Bay opened their eyes—banks of blinking displays and beeping monitors, headsets, and microphones, logistics brains intent on the quiet execution of seven things at once, the closest they had been to a complete air traffic control center on the ground. They knew moving trucks was big business, but they were stunned by the technology behind it all.

What began as a routine benchmarking trip, reviewing providers and their capabilities, became a journey into bigger issues—competitive logistics pressures, strategies and organization structures for success, and above all, winning technologies. Don Schneider offered up some insight about his company's success, "When you think about what we do as a company and why we are so good, two things strike people when they interact with us: First, over the last few years, our strategy has been to invest heavily in technology managing information well. Second, we have some of the best logisticians in the industry with years of experience in optimization and transportation management."

Chris Lofgren, Schneider National's president and CEO, explains what optimization means to truckers. "Our people are experts in figuring out how to deal with a series of constraints that impact solution creation, to satisfy the ultimate needs of the customer, or to take out costs."

Lofgren's team developed and patented some optimization routines that are fast ways to look at huge quantities of data—far faster than any human being can think! The same approach has been used to run manufacturing, where the algorithms have been used to decide how to allocate work to which machines, and how to sequence which activities on which machines to maximize throughput in the factory. The parallel in logistics is to calculate and allocate activities creating the end product. Determine who supplies those services and where they supply them. Here, the objective is to provide on-time services and minimization of costs.

"Logistics," says Lofgren, "is fundamentally the integrating activity of the supply chain. And that's what our business is really about—how do you manage the three flows: the physical flow of the material, the information flow providing visibility, and the funds flow of money between entities."

Schneider Logistics holds patents on another technology tool that produces instant payback, a data manipulation and calculation machine that works from thousands of contract data per second. Understanding the financial implications of contractual factors, such as specifications about how loads are moved, at what price, using which equipment types, and doing it very quickly, has been difficult for customers. "Most people don't have a rating engine that stores these contracts—they will use a generalization," says Lofgren, "but we have the real data. It can all be analyzed, and we can introduce variables that change with every hour. Some people call it an optimization routine, but it isn't because we haven't imposed constraints. It's data manipulation and calculation."

Logistics Paybacks

Lofgren believes that many businesses do not fully understand the impact of logistics costs. "When you look at the macroeconomics of logistics, lots of people fail to realize that between 1981 and now logistics as a percentage of the GNP dropped from 16 percent to less than 10 percent today. That shows there was a fantastic improvement in productivity, a lot of it a result of customers working with providers such as Schneider Logistics to improve the supply chain." Lofgren believes there were many pragmatic solutions at work, as well as optimization models and effectiveness measures. And he noted that the ratio of business inventory to gross national product (GNP) changed, "In 1983 business had to carry 24 percent of the GNP, total investment; that number dropped to 17 percent, just from methodically working with the supply chain to improve on-time delivery."

Looking ahead, Schneider and Lofgren see changes enabled by technology offering even more opportunities for paybacks to smart customers and providers. Lofgren sees logistics providers as a growing impact. "People will create networks allowing them to collaborate and achieve visibility that enables them to be more responsive to their customers' needs. The supply chain is just an extension of the factory with more people who need to collaborate. Any system that's effective will be built around a business process that people can work in. We know it's the systems and the business processes that work together, and the Web provides the mechanism—we had EDI before, but it's the Web that allows people to run applications."

The Schneider business model means participating at a high level and understanding how to bring best practices and strong capabilities into a company. Schneider and Lofgren caution that what is important for companies that want to go after a big logistics payback is a willingness to look at the reality of where their costs are and work together to take inefficiencies out.

Schneider and Lofgren caution against a siloed approach, however. In fact, one of the challenges of companies getting to the next level, like the manufacturing innovators who started out with design for manufacturability (DFM) and cycle time reduction, was not to approach the solution machine by machine, or product by product, not even just across the company. This work has to be done across the supply chain—its about getting your arms around the whole network. "We have the people and the tools to get our arms around the enterprise," said Lofgren.

Lofgren sees the challenge to enlist people who can think about win-win solutions. "There aren't any companies today that can ignore profits. Everybody is being pushed to be more effective. Providers must ask: 'What's the win here for my customer?' I want people who can answer that question working for me. We spend a lot of time at work, and we want bright and capable people creating solutions that excite our customers."

Lofgren believes you can see the difference. "You can walk into an organization, and you can feel how it is working—people are comfortable, they are thinking, they are hustling, they have a sense of purpose, and they know why they are there, you can feel it."

One other software tool offers significant paybacks for logistics and distribution, and that is simulation. The difference between simulation and optimization is the difference between letting a system run and changing the result. Simulation is a descriptive tool and optimization is a prescriptive tool; a simulation routine will describe a system and let it run, while optimization is used to exercise, or improve, a system. Let's say you want to do a network design that determines where the nodes and the distribution centers go. You already know where your plants and customers are, so there are hundreds of possible locations for DCs. It's time to simplify, to make some assumptions. You will want to test them, to see if conditions change or are variable every week, so we simulate the system because we simply cannot check tens of thousands of designs. For two or three scenarios, simulation is a great tool to sharpen or tweak an existing design.

But optimization is much more important and powerful. Simulation will show, once a design exists, how it will behave under certain conditions. Optimization paybacks are big; companies are buying better, keeping less inventory, using fewer people. In fact, in the aggregate, optimized procurement saves 10 to 15 percent on transportation expenditures. Systems performing auto dispatching produce 10 percent right at the start. Soft-side benefits add up to paybacks as well. Trucking companies that optimize their schedules reduce driver turnover by 30 to 40 percent because the best way to keep employees is to get them home at a reasonable hour. In the trucking industry turnover is high, and every year it costs five to ten thousand dollars to train each replacement to be a good driver. But when schedulers can reduce empty miles by 20 percent or more, and increase the level of service as well, it means drivers get home more often.

Although we are just in the infancy of these powerful tools, the next big advance will be collaborative commerce driven by tools that will work across companies, so that they can plan more, optimize better, and develop greater visibility. Although the tools to run joint procurement, using a company's truck for instance, are available, the barriers are more mind-set—worries about data security for instance, and until people get more comfortable with the technology, some new approaches will take time for adoption.

"It's like the Web security question, people get over it. It's inevitable—there will, of course, be industry-wide networks because the whole idea in logistics is to collaborate." A closed system won't help companies deal with the outside world. "For logistics to work, the more open the system, the better it is."

Not all organizations should immediately adopt advanced software tools like optimization and simulation, however. The first step of some companies is simply to improve processes, take out waste, and find out where the money goes. In logistics and distribution, functions that have always occupied lower levels on the prestige ladder, smart managers are discovering that huge amounts of cash can be freed up just by mapping and studying the network. For companies like John Deere, which grew up decentralized, the unmined payback treasure simply opens the eyes of nonbelievers. When Deere took a good look at its logistics and distribution costs, the company realized that injecting only a few different approaches would quickly yield good results, operationally and financially.

Out of Deere's total yearly $7 billion spend, logistics and distribution accounted for nearly 10 percent, or $600 to $700 million, but planners were unclear exactly how that tab broke down. Management wanted to see savings, but they had no idea where to start. With dozens of plants worldwide making their own shipping arrangements, there was a feeling that the company wasn't leveraging its logistics spend. Smaller Deere plants on their own were little fish to the big steamship or trucking lines; but by gathering a few of the plants together, the fish got bigger, and so did the savings. Estimates of potential savings ranged from $10 million the first year to $60 million in three years.

First off, planners mapped out Deere's worldwide logistics/distribution system, seeking to identify strategic areas with heavy logistics volumes. For Deere, one heavy area was Wisconsin, where suppliers needed a consolidation point. Another area was Northern Italy. Working from the process maps, planners were able to describe the baseline by identifying specifically what parts shipped from where to where.

The next steps included locating cross-docks to strategically serve all of Deere from local suppliers. Next came financial controls to nail down the money flows; and the final step, software systems, promised even bigger paybacks. With a clean process, software systems can make great inroads; for example, two well-trained transportation planners might take sixteen staff hours to develop outbound truckloads for each day's schedule. Software takes that workload down to about one half hour, minus human computing errors. That move alone took several million dollars out of the process.

Some Toyota Production System advocates miss the necessity of using software tools to manage large complex networks, especially the ones running automotive and electronics pipelines across the United States. It is nearly impossible, however, as even Toyota's inventory figures prove, to manage such a system without software assists. Inventory turns, the key metric tracked by Richard Schonberger, the Seattle-based consultant who brought Japanese manufacturing techniques to North America, illustrates this fact. While Toyota revenues grew 12.5 percent to $126 billion, with profits climbing 31 percent to $5.1 billion in fiscal 2002, inventories went in the other direction; turns peaked in the late 1970s and early 1980s at 60 and higher, but they fell to 11.3 in 2002.[3]

The United States is about three thousand miles long, with diverse business cultures from the thousands of border *maqui-*

lladora in El Paso to the revitalized Rust Belt cities, with incredible weather shifts thrown in. It takes good data and good manipulation capabilities to keep that pipeline running lean. Good software planning and execution, plus communication tools are an absolute necessity.

Software tools can do more than help design and locate better distribution networks. The best packages will help to identify critical parts that must move in the pipelines to maintain just-in-time schedules, and those parts that can be easily inventoried for high service requirements. The software enables planners to plan and understand how much these material management decisions truly cost.

And what was Deere's payback? Planners beat the target the first year and saved $13 million. With the addition of big guns software, managers projected $30 million savings in three years from a $2.5 million systems investment, a twelve-fold payback. The goal was $20 million per year, over seventy Deere factories worldwide.

Building Partnership Trust and Communications Flows

In the early 1990s, suppliers were inundated with well-meaning customer audits. Sometimes the multiple demands of different customers caused confusion at plant sites that were already pressed with technical and delivery demands. Suppliers wondered if customers knew what impact their audits were actually having on performance, and they needed a credible feedback device. Motorola, Honda, and other companies responded to this cry for help with their supplier surveys, documents administered by third-party neutral groups. The surveys were designed to elicit useful information with the right amount of detail that would cause customers to ask the right questions, and help suppliers do the best job they could. The survey became an annual event for many customers, and findings caused further modifications as particular problems became clearer.

We think this is an invaluable tool to building a strong supply base. The idea is to give suppliers all the useful information they need, in the form they need it, to do the absolute best job they can for customers.

Honda discovered an unexpected benefit from this survey. As customers and suppliers dialogue about key questions, they start to refine their communication flows and develop common definitions of objective and goals. The survey becomes more than a feedback tool when it begins to launch strategic planning reviews.

There's More . . .

Helping suppliers reduce costs and improve processes and products is just one high payback practice among the twenty we highlighted in *The Purchasing Machine*. Other approaches to supply management and Spend Management emphasize the same Incredible Payback objectives, and they take producers beyond exciting kaizen methods into bigger and longer-lasting gains (see Figure 4–2). DuPont, one of our favorite Best Practice innovators, offers a unique approach to The Incredible Payback, one that takes a wider, global view of the supply base.

DuPont's 3X Challenge

Beyond pioneering lean results, there are many strategies available to take eager supply operations farther. What our early work with kaizen proved was that if suppliers could realize enormous productivity gains one time on individual lines, at individual plants, the potential for enterprise-wide gains was staggering. Paybacks need not be confined to production processes, as Dupont's Henri Irrthum, vice president and chief procurement officer, knows. Irrthum explained the company's 3X test, a unique approach that guarantees payback for every dollar invested in procurement.

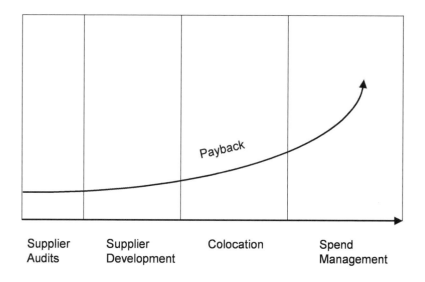

| Supplier Audits | Supplier Development | Colocation | Spend Management |

Figure 4–2. Working with the supply base.

Irrthum directs DuPont's $17 billion annual spend within some unique cost justification parameters. Every project and every personnel expenditure for his operation must pass the 3X Payback Test. The 3X Payback Test is a basic rule of thumb, a multiplier, that requires the sourcing operation to deliver, on average, savings that are equal to three to four times its total cost. For example, if a procurement department costs $100 million a year in total costs—not only personnel costs but also the work procurement does, including telephone, office space, travel salaries, health benefits—then that department under Irrthum's 3X Payback Test must deliver three to four times total costs, or $300 to $400 million in net savings per year.

"The savings have to be repeated to stay in business," says Irrthum, "and these are net savings. We have a pretty tough definition of net savings. They don't include cost avoidances, for instance. If the market for a commodity goes up by 10 percent, and then you take 4 percent off that market base, the savings don't count toward the multiplier because your savings need to come in below the market. It's a pretty tough target—the CEO is not concerned with currency fluctuations that go against you—'that's just too bad!'" explains Irrthum.

How does Irrthum's 3X Payback Test come into play for supplier relationship management? Supplier relationship management, especially the development phase, is people intensive—it doesn't happen without dedication of good, well-prepared purchasing experts. Budgeting for new personnel falls into the 3X category if, according to Irrthum, "you can say 'I will save three to four times that person's total cost, for that project', well, you have a very good chance that the request for two or three more people will be approved because you know and you can prove that they will deliver at least four times their total cost in savings."

Furthermore, Irrthum's approach guarantees quick decisions because the groundwork is already laid for a positive result. "The project must be well-defined" he warns, "not fuzzy—hard communication with numbers, not soft arguments." Although customers may want to help suppliers improve because it is "the right thing to do," for intensive customer involvement the numbers have to make sense as well.

Sourcing and Logistics—The Land of Opportunity!

Dupont's approach, Irrthum further explains, is another indicator of the company's commitment to a "data driven—not opinion-driven—Six Sigma philosophy. Year to year," says Irrthum, "the opportunities vary. Sourcing and logistics is the land of opportunity!"

Irrthum advises maintaining a broad, global focus: "Look at the moment in time and ask, 'How well have we worked in the past in this area?' You need to look at the supply base and ask, 'Has that changed?' Look more global rather than regional, and you must look at more low-cost countries." The horizon opens up more every day; although the competitive situation among suppliers might change, "new opportunities exist all the time—there are mergers, acquisitions, diversification in our industry in the supply base. There are people who disappear from the customer's horizon, or there are new ones coming on." And on the supply side there are more suppliers coming from Asia or Eastern Europe, for example, so Irrthum advises looking there for technology and quality even before it is approved, and there are still more opportunities: "It's every CPO's dream. You can't stand still."

"Is There Another Deal That We Can Make Better Than We Did Yesterday?"

Taking a wider perspective toward your competitive position in Spend Management, DuPont's Irrthum agrees, means looking at the entire industry for competitive benchmarks. Irrthum cites the example of the telecom industry. Telecom prices illustrate dramatic shifts as technologies improved and the supply base grew. Although the first cell phones cost hundreds of dollars, the next one was a better deal, until the price dropped to the level of disposables.

"There was always a better deal the next time, and the price never stopped dropping. You need to make sure you are on the forefront of those changes. If you don't, you won't stay competitive. Keep a 360-degree view all the time, be awake to not miss any opportunities, and make sure you keep your company best in class. It's not easy," he believes, "because the world's possibilities are getting bigger, and traditionally we may not have tapped into all the possibilities around the world, but they are definitely becoming more available this time. Stay with it and don't be satisfied."

In the telecommunications market, for example, a buyer may have gotten a 30 percent price reduction at one moment, and thought that was great! Irrthum warns that: "In another couple of months, you can get another 20 percent or so. Never be satisfied, even if you did in fact bring in savings bigger than the previous year's, that is only one vector. You need to stay ahead of the competition, or at least even with them, and make sure that whatever you buy is hopefully better than what your competition buys."

How They Do It

Supplier development is a proven approach to finding big paybacks throughout the supply base. And the simplest way to capture these gains is to work the numbers at all levels of the supply chain. Companies like Honda of America, Deere, and Delphi first identify key suppliers, a manageable group with whom the customer maintains good relationships, communications, and trust. These companies become partners with whom they plan to grow together.

Next, they then work with those selected suppliers to track quality, cost, and delivery performance to identify improvement opportunities. The objective is for both the customer and the supplier to make a fair profit; reaching a detailed understanding of a supplier's process and technology, its costs and problems, is the first step to improvement.

But what are the options if your organization is dealing at arm's length with hundreds of relatively unknown suppliers? Can big companies with extended supply chains deliver the kind of Incredible Payback that keeps suppliers as developing partners, rather than cost-cutting targets? It all comes down to management philosophy, advises coauthor Nelson. When CEOs decide to maintain an enterprise of committed, exclusive (or nearly exclusive) suppliers, their ongoing costs and new product introduction record reflects that commitment. But when top executives do not understand, or fail to recognize the importance of a strong supply base, the job of supply managers becomes less strategic and more tactical. And the supply base inevitably becomes a revolving door.

Don't Underestimate Supplier Development Expertise!

Investments in supplier development and supply base management yield huge payoffs. At Deere and Delphi, a $100,000 investment in one supplier development engineer often yields from three to ten times the original investment. Top performers can achieve even more, truly an example of an Incredible Payback.

When companies outsource a high percentages of purchased parts, the requirement to carefully target supplier management and development methods becomes critical. In the automotive industry, for example, where final assembly plants receive hourly shipments of seat systems, dashboards, fuel systems, and even tires, excellent supplier communications and performance is a necessity. At one transplant assembly plant, the cost of line-down (stoppage for shortages or quality issues) is $26,000 *per minute*. It's easy to see why this producer maintains a staff of engineers and planners, one to one, for its key suppliers.

But beyond the investment in supplier development resources, The Incredible Payback takes a strategic approach to decisions that set up financial returns for years to come. When Delphi decided to rationalize its supply base and save millions of dollars annually, the company organized the global sourcing function to look beyond supplier development or performance issues. The targets became bigger and more sustained.

Supplier surveys, open-book accounting, *jikons* (Japanese-style customer/supplier meetings), just-in-time and lean manufacturing, as well as innovative new product development approaches are just a few supplier management tools that yield Incredible Payback.

Motorola Perspective

Theresa Metty, the senior chief procurement officer of Motorola, places her trust in a few supplier management tools: total purchased cost, technology and market trends, and a drive to reduce the cost of complexity. For Metty, whose career path has covered manufacturing, purchasing, and accounting executive roles, making tough decisions in the telecom industry has been facilitated by paying attention to big, big numbers.

Furthermore, because Metty had responsibility for manufacturing as well as purchasing at Motorola, she could weigh internal production costs and decisions against Spend Management principles, especially outsourcing decisions. Metty believes, for instance, that many outsourcing decisions made by manufacturing personnel carry bad investment returns, and that they were made primarily to guarantee no interruptions of deliveries. She believes that better deals now await the sharp purchasing analyst.

And so her overwhelming view to the numbers means that in an operation that honors innovation and variety, she tasks purchasing planners with the goal of running their businesses like commodity markets. Despite the high degree of innovation Motorola cellular engineers bring to every new product, Metty is looking for economies in purchasing that yield competitive pricing and significant paybacks. If an internal supplier does not measure up to Motorola's competition on price, quality, or features, or if she believes that parts standardization will take another two or three percentage points off the component price, she expects her people to do it.

Taking a commodity approach in an innovation market has allowed Metty to cut costs and continue to introduce many new products and features every year, despite strong global competition. Commodity management, or thinking like a commodity trader, requires fierce devotion to the numbers, and an immediate response when one metric gets out of line because in big integrated enterprises, the impact is wide and immediate.

Bringing Your Partners into the Game

The gains (and the losses) cascade quickly throughout the enterprise as pricing, cost overruns, and consolidation of savings accumulate. Mark Preston, manager of supplier development at Respironics, a company at the beginning of a new approach to supply chain management, instituted the following five key performance measures with its top twenty-three suppliers, companies that represent 50 percent of the company's total spend:

1. Inventory turns
2. Quality ppm
3. Purchased dollars compared year to year
4. ISO
5. Percent of revenue Respironics represents to the supplier

Tracking just these few key metrics allowed Respironics to focus on a promising supplier with a big quality problem. Often, customers find themselves tied to suppliers whether things are going well or not, and Preston took on the role of project leader to identify and launch continuous improvement projects for a handful of struggling suppliers. Respironics's 25 percent growth rate would not wait, and Preston knew that he had to get the word out fast that one way or the other, Respironics needed its partners to find better ways to grow with them.

At one East coast supplier, for instance, the company found two key production processes were failing under pressures of high-volume growth demands. It is not uncommon for innovative small suppliers to struggle with outdated production or distribution processes inherited from their first generation founders. Preston called in a Honda BP veteran, Dave Curry, to help identify and organize solutions.

Thirteen weeks later, Curry's team delivered an amazing tally of Phase I results, from 5S cleanup and reorganization and cells out on the shop floor to root cause analysis that pointed out a desperate need to automate processes that were not robust enough for Respironics's quality standards. Initial capacity analysis eliminated the need for a fifth production line, and 5S reorganizing of line flows cut inventories as well.

With seven years of history behind Respironics and this key supplier, it was important to determine where the limits of the partnership would lie given continuous high-growth projections. Sound payback numbers proved that for an investment of thirteen weeks' team time and some outside help, clear opportunities immediately appeared as low-hanging fruit, and quickly recaptured the initial investment. Further improvements in automation and quality would require more root cause analysis and some limited capital equipment investment, cost-justified by potential savings as well as the cost of quality benefits.

Phase I results brought team members a few surprises. The biggest Incredible Payback, a 27 percent production increase, solved a nagging backorder problem. There had never been enough capacity, enough throughput, pre-BP project, to ship all customer orders complete and on time. In fact, this item had been in backorder for about a year and a half. The backorder position was quickly eliminated, and stayed that way. Planners point to communication changes that contributed to this solution. Customer/supplier reports, up to 25 different ones, flew back and forth as planners attempted to track and move backordered units, but Curry's team consolidated the information into one powerful document. Now all staff members know where they stand and when to produce, what, and how.

Backorders were hurting international customers especially. One huge overseas order worth $1.5 million sat waiting for eighty units. International orders must ship complete, so they often linger while waiting for missing pieces. After the team completed Phase I, planners were able to identify this type of order before it entered production, plan for it, and ship on time and complete.

Team members proudly point to one extra achievement: On top of meeting their high-growth customer's demand spikes, they were able to increase yields by another 5 percent.

Respironics planners became so convinced of the power of supplier development after piloting with one supplier, they quickly moved on to an injection molder and a plastic extrusion producer. They issued the World-Class Supplier Challenge, a competition in which each key supplier reported on what it had accomplished on world-class practices. A team of judges drawn from operations judged the entries, with the winner slated for a World-Class Supplier trophy to be awarded at the next supplier day.

Early Partners in Sensible Design Savings

Tracking key operating performance measures, like quality ppm and scrap costs, is great for products in full production, but what about bringing supplier partners into the game during early design and prototype stages, when 90 percent of the cost of new products and much of the manufacturing quality challenge is committed? Most companies still have difficulty joining engineering with buying functions, and few systems offer the kind of information required by both sides to understand and plan for each other's parameters. Cost savings to procurement from standardizing parts lists, for instance, is something every operation wants, but most still find it difficult to achieve. The best time to involve buyers in the design cycle, however, is at the very beginning, not after a product has ramped up. With good systems to help purchasing and engineering, staffers can be brought together early in the design cycle by colocation, but this requires deliberate attention to setting goals that work for both functions. Harley-Davidson is an example of a well-established giant that has polished its engineering/procurement skills. New product launches, like the Softail, are design and process breakthroughs for engineering as well as purchasing.

Put More Purchasing into Engineering, and More Engineers into Purchasing!

One approach to achieving clear financial payback is to reduce product complexity, especially the number of nonstandard parts, that engineers ask purchasing to buy. And the most obvious approach to reducing parts proliferation is to limit the number of suppliers—two or three key suppliers are more apt to work from the same parts list than dozens of suppliers, all dealing with varying volumes and life cycles. Mike Polcari, vice president of IBM procurement engineering, is an integrator whose team works with IBM designers and suppliers to help them create the right technology at the right time. Polcari brings seemingly different interests together and works at creating what IBM calls *technology convergence.* He lists technology forums as one approach to helping purchasing engineers work convergence issues with suppliers.[4]

IBM's technology forum, designed by former CPO Gene Richter, was the ideal place to discuss where products are going technically, and what suppliers' perspectives are on new technologies. These open discussions created trust, identified problems, and helped reduce costs while partners get to market quicker than their competition. These meetings also allowed IBM to have influence early on in suppliers' technology directions.

Procurement engineers can work to move suppliers away from difficult or dying technologies, but they should also move the industry toward standard, rather than proprietary, parts. Reducing the variety in battery types in cell phones, for instance, saves customers money as it makes purchasing's job easier. Cell phone customers, of course, find it easier and cheaper to have fewer types of replacement batteries.

According to Lucent Technologies' Jose Mejia, president of the company's supply chain network organization, his group does more than direct designers to preferred suppliers. They look at supplier reuse and other issues that cover design of the supply chain itself. Mejia believes Lucent's supply chain innovation is paying off with better product margins created by lower product costs.

Complexity in old and new products costs money. Motorola's Personal Communications Sector under CPO Theresa Metty (vice president of worldwide supply chain at the time) led her team to savings of more than a billion dollars, much of which she attributes to component reuse, postponement, and use of industry standard parts in products they design. She is confident that's only the beginning.

In the electronic management services world, where contract manufacturing experts take on billions of dollars of outsourced products—from design and assembly, all the way through logistics and delivery—innovation brings better and cheaper launches. John Sammut, president and CEO of Epic Technologies of Rochester, Michigan, has come up with an innovative approach to customer/supplier partnering that eliminates hand-offs and cuts supplier development costs. Sammut's method also speeds product launches, which are so critical to electronics contract success.

EPIC's Customer Focus Team, Colocation and Beyond!

The idea grew out of continuous improvement work that Sammut's group has done with several customers. In 2002, Epic launched a new plant in Juarez, Mexico. Three months into the launch, the plant was producing higher yields at 5 percent lower costs for circuit boards in the continuous positive airway pressure (CPAP)—a sleep apnea product—product line. Sammut believes that what made this launch smoother than usual was the customer focus team from EPIC's Norwalk, Ohio, operation who traveled to Mexico and helped set up, train, document, and do first article approvals on the Juarez product.

The team included a process engineer, test engineer, material analyst, quality engineer, an account manager, and inside sales, all from Ohio. The team conducted weekly reviews with the customer on all critical metrics: on-time delivery, inventory turns, yields by product, as well as quality and flow issues. Sammut recalls, "When we really started to focus on quality, we found lots of test correlation problems. Products might pass our test, but not theirs, or there were different tests. We closed the gaps and our yields rose from ppm in the 30K range, down to 8K in nine months—we knew then we were down to the real quality problems! We've eliminated the noise, and what we learned from the test correlation problems we applied to new product development teams to improve customer design for manufacturability (DFM) and design for testability (DFT) reviews. On some of the more recent product releases that we 'codeveloped' with much more early involvement, our yields further improved with ppms in the 2–3K range of launch.

"It's a big change in the partnership," says Sammut, "as we get more involved in the design cycle. In the past, we might not see our customers' designs until they came to us for a quote—'Hey, here's a concept, and here are the schematics!'" Now, the supplier helps the customers lay out the products and select components to avoid obsolescence or design in an alternative to achieve the same functionality at lower cost. And the payback for the customer focus intensive approach? Epic saved its customers $2.5 million on annualized production of $30 million, which was an 8 percent cost reduction.

But wait, there's more! From Ohio to Mexico, next stop China! Using the customer focus team to participate in design and bring up full production is a concept that can help consolidate the supply base as it is applied to more customers.

"We do more with fewer customers, so there is a concentration issue that comes up," says Sammut. For example, one North American customer that maintains an injection-molding facility in China is introducing a new, very small, high-volume automotive product. The customer wants to outsource every part of production, including the final integration that would normally be completed in China. That's another handoff, and possibly an additional cost. Epic's novel solution? Launch the product locally, using the Norwalk, Ohio facility to do NPI services—process development, prototype builds, DFT, DFM, and product validation and approval for volume. Then, produce the product in volume in Mexico for the first six months, until processes are stable and volumes take off. Next, take the work cell and a handful of Juarez employees, along with the customer focus team, on the road to China.

The transplant group stays in China for three to six months to train the Asian workforce and to locate production inside the customer's facility—a nod to colocation—and bingo, product is now tested and approved, and is coming from the lowest-cost production area. Sammut believes this novel approach can produce significant savings, because "higher risk yields higher rewards, because the customer has consolidated suppliers to one source, and cut new product introduction time and cost by eliminating heavy supplier development expenses in China" (see Figure 4–3).

Sammut's $5.33 million savings estimate relies heavily on building volume as the China plant continues to deliver lower costs. An additional payback, over one half million, derives from Epic-negotiated component cost savings; when customers outsource production to electronic management services suppliers, they should obtain better component prices at the same time, and Sammut's model includes this approach.

Conclusion

There is a progression of involvement by customers in supplier work, from simply demanding compliance to customer quality standards, and auditing to enforce it, to full-blown partnering for design and manufacturing process-sharing. Each approach has a potentially significant payoff when it is well executed. It is important before jumping into supplier development, however, to set a limit on the investment and to get expert help to protect projected

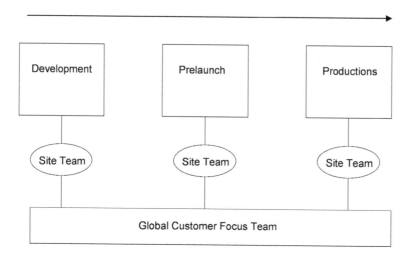

Figure 4-3. Product life cycle.

paybacks. Every project proposed to improve processes will not have the same payback, and not every project needs to be tackled at the beginning of the journey—save some work for more seasoned team members.

For more experienced supply managers, like those at John Deere, individual projects offer nearly unlimited cost savings opportunities in surprising areas. Traditional products manufacturing, like shims at the Horicon plant, produced 14 percent cost reductions; a $7 million investment in supplier development yielded over $22 million in savings, three times the original investment. Even the area of indirect materials continues to offer most companies enormous opportunities. For Deere, indirect materials produced over $17 million in savings in a single year.

The bar continues to move higher and higher, as model performers like Honda and Toyota perfect the capabilities of their supply base stars. Toyota, for example, has announced a new strategic imperative—to hold 15 percent of worldwide market share, with 30 percent annual cost down. For companies just getting started on supply management best practices, that's a tough act to follow!

Notes

1. "Executive Report of Key Results of Recent Research on Supplier Development Strategies and Outcomes," a whitepaper prepared by Dr. Robert Handfield, Director, Supply Chain Resource Consortium, North Carolina State University College of Management, for Jonathan Stegner, p. 2.
2. Anthony C. Laraia, Patricia E. Moody and Robert W. Hall, *The Kaizen Blitz, Accelerating Breakthroughs in Productivity and Performance* (New York: John Wiley & Sons, 1999), p. 189.
3. David Drickhamer, "Inventory Bloat at Toyota, What Gives?" *Industry Week* online, June 12, 2003.
4. Jim Carbone, "Involve Buyers!" *Purchasing*, March 31, 2002 (Purchasing.com).

Chapter 5

Developing Incredible Payback People, Organizations, and Systems

Purchasing operations and people have changed significantly in the last five to ten years. The name, the goals, the organizational structure, and more important, the compensation for supply management professionals reflect progress and greater opportunities.

But many procurement professionals trace their careers back to buyer/planner positions for which, unfortunately, few buyers were required to develop in-depth expertise on supplier processes or technologies and manufacturing methods. The supply base was a wide assortment of individual suppliers, some of whom might not have been heard from in years. The role of purchasing buyers was more limited and their evaluations hinged on tough cost negotiations. Now, however, supply management professionals find themselves at the head of the enterprise, overlooking a long line of operations where anything can go wrong, and many areas for significant improvements lie waiting for discovery. The opportunity to have an impact on real profits and strategic initiatives is there for new supply management professionals who are prepared, ready, and in the right kind of organizational structure.

Even the look of the supply management function has changed because new supply management structures, responsibilities, and information flows have appeared in the past five years—collaborations, consortia, supplier councils, matrixed groups, and commodity teams. All of this means that supply chain careers offer more choices in compensation, training, and communications, plus visibility is high.

Training, compensation, organizational structure, and even office location have opened up. Higher-paid and better-prepared professionals are more ready to take on management responsibilities at all points in the supply chain—from new product design to logistics and distribution. We believe that now is a great time to be a supply chain professional, because as one of the few corporate contributors who can deliver paybacks in the three-, four-, five-, and even ten-fold range, purchasing matters. Supply management investments in people, processes, and systems have a great payback.

In this chapter, we look at examples of tools and Best Practice models to help companies move from traditional procurement to Incredible Payback supply chains. The first step is to get information: See what's out there, what works, and why. Next, compare this information with the current operation, looking for gaps and problem areas. Finally, we urge supply chain managers looking to start making significant paybacks relatively soon to beef up supplier capabilities, computer systems, and lean methods, and to take a good look at optimizing organizational structures. In the short-term, the examples and ideas we provide will produce good immediate payback; but in the long-term, bigger challenges like organizational restructuring will take more time and focus.

Reaching for The Incredible Payback

How many corporate investments in people, new systems, equipment, even training, carry real payoffs three, four, five or even ten times their original investment cost? Not possible you say? Yet, these solutions are exactly what most companies need—not layoffs and cost-cutting drives—to carry them through this tough economy. And evaluating every new training program, every new hire, even software program as to its projected returns by asking, "Does this pass The Incredible Payback test?" is after all not such a crazy idea. It's what Wall Street does every day. It's why we start companies and why we periodically restructure—we are always looking for that big return.

Incredible Payback solutions are those powerful and sensible ideas that yield strong results—their applications meet the promise, and remarkably, many big solutions require only common sense. Subjecting an organization or an idea to The Incredible Payback test means that no action is taken to change an operation unless it is certain to produce high yields. Leading companies put every decision, each proposed project, even outsourcing, through a payback test.

The Outsourced Payback

In our complex supply chains, the success of the first tier is largely dependent on second-, third-, and even fourth-tier suppliers. Yet North American end producers cannot legally form *kieretsu* (Japanese industry groups), one approach to guaranteeing performance from suppliers; nor can they buy out or take a controlling interest in every critical supplier in the supply base. Instead, they typically outsource to the real experts, the small- and medium-size producers of tooling, stampings, plastic injection parts, and electronic components, each representing a very different technology. Many companies struggle with the trade-offs of outsourcing, however, because however convenient it has become, it is not a perfect solution.

The advantages of outsourcing to the experts, however—especially in pricing and flexibility—can be outweighed by quality and delivery challenges, especially in young suppliers. The answer, coauthor Nelson believes, and the one that his team practiced well and thoroughly at his previous employer, Honda of America, is a big payback solution—investment in supply management engineers, a new breed of manufacturing/purchasing professionals. Supply management professionals anticipate, intervene, fix, and help suppliers correct bad processes and improve quality, delivery, and price. The typical 100K per year investment in a top supply management engineer quickly pays off in savings three times or more: Best results are ten times initial investment.

And there is a new paradigm at work here. The approach is to eliminate waste in all areas and share the results. Both elements are necessary to motivate exceptional results.

Similarly, Honda suppliers recorded big payback improvements in ppm and supplier deliveries as they focused hard on metrics and root cause projects in a host of supplier seminars and training, thereby slashing quality defects tenfold, from 1,500 defects in 1987 to just over 100 in 1996; on-time deliveries rose from 97 percent to 99 percent on time, the absolute minimum for sound JIT operations.

Building a strong supplier development capability is not the only road to The Incredible Payback operation, however. Leveraged technology, smart software solutions, is also an approach well used by a few supply chain innovators like Buell Motorcycle.

Buell Motorcycle's 10X Solution

Sometimes 10X yields appear from simple systems innovations like Buell Motorcycle's parts system, an off-the-shelf package that allows Buell and supplier engineers to design parts and track costs and revisions live online, with everyone seeing and maintaining the same parts data. It's a great system because of its simplicity and power. It's a big payback solution and it's growable.

Pop-open windows reach deeper into the part history and provide detailed explanations of any deviations from the plan. Freeing up program managers from translation, data collection, and integration of disparate parts cost and quality control historical data is an Incredible Payback solution—the payoffs with live products are huge. Ease of connectivity enables service folks to tie into the Buell engineering team. Enabling parallel supplier and assembler work teams means the designs will be quite robust for service and when the system is expanded a little further, direct communication of field issues to a supplier after the vehicle is in production. A 10X solution delivers 10X savings on aftermarket costs.

Evaluate the Payback

Improvements that consistently yield hard savings make their way to the bottom line, and into next year's purchasing budgets. Even though capital investment formulas, however, might require payoff justifications in the big payback range, not all capital investments in equipment, systems, and so forth truly ever deliver all the promised yields. How many times have your plant engineers calculated big returns on a new machine investment, only to fall short of breakeven because volumes never developed? Or, has your company learned about the "real" cost of a blind Internet auction bid? Used properly, an auction is an effective tool, but it's not the only tool in the box!

When times are tough, line item scrutiny dogs budget meetings, and painful as that exercise may be, big payback winners prove that passing every new idea through the payback test—"Will this person or system or new machine tool produce three-, four-, or five-fold returns?"—is worth it. If the answer is yes, do it; if the answer is immeasurable or unclear, defer. But first ask the payback question to evaluate the project's potential payback.

We like to think that supply chain executives who understand the exponential financial returns—yields that we call Incredible Paybacks—and how to get them, are the upcoming winners in the extended enterprise. Although many organizations would love to have high-yield managers and teams, only a handful of bright stars have achieved this kind of return. Yet, as companies like Honda, Deere, Delphi, and their suppliers have proven, Best Practices and payback analysis offer incredible opportunities.

The Incredible Payback

How to save bi$$ions without laying off millions

Combined with Best Practices yields 3, 5, 7X per year savings

Steps:

Centralize

Leverage the buy

Be your supplier's best customer

Stars: Honda, Delphi, Deere, and new software innovators

Benchmarking to Minimize Evaluation Risk

One way to look at the new methods from a safe distance, before jumping into major change and investment outlays, is to observe and study the models. Pioneers in new manufacturing methods have been doing intensive benchmarking for about twenty years, since the first "journeys to the gemba," the Kawasaki plant in Nebraska, that started the whole lean pilgrimage. Benchmarking trips to Japan and transplant operations in North America to observe best practice manufacturing sites gave kaizen pioneers an upfront, real understanding of early Japanese manufacturing systems, and we recommend talking and looking at good supply chain operations the same way.

Talk with the best-of-the-best customers and suppliers alike—supply management change agents need to see both sides of the fence—to understand what really works well, and what doesn't. It is, however, more difficult to benchmark purchasing operations than to tour a manufacturing line or cell, because it is difficult to learn everything about leveraging a supply chain from simply observing a good one in action. Visiting supplier plant sites tells much, but to really understand purchasing effectiveness, benchmarkers need to look at performance numbers as well. Many tasks in supply chain departments are white-collar "thinking" jobs that require analysis and communications, and these activities are harder to observe in action. The sixty-thousand-member Institute for Supply Management (formerly NAPM), especially its Web site (http://www.ism.ws/), the Center for Advanced Purchasing Management (CAPS) research programs, and ISM's flagship publication *Inside Supply Management* are great starting points.

There are other data rich opportunities to learn from the best and the worst, and one is Dr. Robert Monczka's landmark research study, the 10X Project.

The 10X Project—From Observations, a Road Map

For more than seven years, Dr. Robert Monczka of Michigan State and the Institute of Supply Management has led a massive research project to define purchasing progress. Monczka's goal, to build a model that would allow purchasing pros to self-assess their operations' maturity level and set goals for improvement in specific areas, uncovered and gathered a wealth of data from which any purchasing operation can learn.

Monczka worked with more than 250 companies, mostly Fortune 200 to 500, to establish emerging sourcing and supply chain strategies, and explain how performance improvements of five to ten times (10X) can be achieved over the next five years and beyond. A series of visioning workshops, a Delphi study, and other research form the basis of the project work, which has taken seven years and nine full-time people to build.

The 10X Project is designed to provide an integrated and coherent vision across industries, to identify Best Practices, and to provide road maps from current to future Best Practices. For example, the study includes a clear model on organizational structure—not totally centralized, but supported by commodity teams that are led by a central procurement expert. The teams are made up of purchasing people from all over the world, and together they make decisions on where to place new business.

The 10X Project's results can be used to help companies establish, enhance, and deploy leading-edge sourcing and supply chain strategies and practices worldwide, enabling world-class performance improvements of up to ten times. One observation from the study is that supply chain strategies will directly contribute to improvement in a firm's economic picture. Other macro scenarios will continue to develop and have an impact on the development of new business, sourcing and supply chain strategies three and more years out.

Specifically, the project identifies six macro environment scenarios to watch for:[1]

1. The financial community will continue to pressure companies for improved short-term financial performance.
2. Supply chains are reforming into customer focused virtual networks.
3. Increased competition and globalization is driving development of newer and more innovative processes and technologies to develop and deliver new products, services, and total solutions to customers faster and with more value.
4. Continuous real-time global connectivity to provide cross-

enterprise information transparency and the ability to quickly respond to economic changes on a worldwide basis.

5. The need for skilled human capital is forcing radical changes in work environment, acquisition and development of personnel skills, and organizational structure.

6. Realized innovation and accelerated implementation will provide firms the basis for achieving sustainable competitive advantage.

Using 10X to Ratchet Up Performance

Beth Heinrich, Motorola 10X Project user, likes being able to use the system to compare her semiconductor results to those from other companies. "There's a wealth of information going back to the early and mid-1990s for people who want to know road maps, key definitions and terms, and Best Practices, as well as how to get there." Heinrich's area has benchmarked internally as well, using the 10X Assessment Tool to see where Motorola stands on internal product development, by surveying internal partners using some of the 10X Project base questions. Next steps, according to Heinrich, include assessments of commodity/supplier strategic development, structuring and maintaining a world-class supply base, and strategic supplier alliances.

The tool can also be used to complete assessments that compare performance of one commodity team with another or to benchmark different metrics that measure total supply chain effectiveness. Typical benchmarking items include early supplier involvement and metrics that look at supply chain velocities. Heinrich's group is also looking at organizational effectiveness by using 10X to develop its own surveys on commodity strategy development. She believes the 10X data is invaluable, and it is available nowhere else. "Surveys help us identify where we have gaps, or where we do something very well."

First inroads into the 10X database led Heinrich to draw the following four conclusions about lessons learned:

1. It is better to involve more cross-functional team members and partners to get a more realistic assessment.
2. There is a huge amount of information available, and the team felt they needed to identify a way to ramp users up quickly.
3. Users need to follow up with additional assessments over time, to track results, and make strategy corrections.
4. Users need more participation by companies outside Motorola to increase external benchmarking opportunities.

Benchmarking the best, and most thoughtful, observation of available data from the 10X Project is a good preamble to the next big step, laying a Best Practices foundation and building The Incredible Payback operation.

Building the New 10X High-Yield Operation

What combination of people and systems will create the new 10X juggernaut from a traditional purchasing department? Organizations go up and down, but a few notable Best Practice examples continue to shine. We identified ten stars in our 2001 book *The Purchasing Machine*, including American Express, SmithKline Beecham, Daimler Chrysler, Harley-Davidson, Honda of America, IBM, John Deere, Whirlpool, Flextronics, and Sun Microsystems. We also identified twenty Best Practices that mark a great purchasing organization, including:

1. Cost management
2. Supplier development
3. Value analysis, value engineering
4. MRO, indirect, and nontraditional purchasing

5. Supplier quality circles
6. Training
7. Supplier information sharing
8. Supplier conference
9. Supplier performance reporting
10. Supplier surveys
11. Delivery improvement
12. Tool and technical assistance centers
13. Supplier support (SWAT) team
14. Loaned executives
15. Early supplier involvement
16. New model development group
17. Written strategy for every supplier and every part/commodity
18. Strategic planning and administration
19. Career path planning and academic outreach
20. Purchasing systems

And the newest addition to the top twenty,

21. Spend Management

An organization that has all or most of the Best Practices, like Honda of America and IBM purchasing, is an excellent purchasing model. To these twenty Best Practices, we have added the twenty-first, Spend Management, and we now know that Spend Management is what allows companies to leverage their total purchasing spend into savings and profits for the entire company. Although many companies cannot yet point to a systematic Spend Management process, it is the next step they will need to understand and put in place to achieve Incredible Paybacks. They may actually be applying a few pieces of Spend Management, such as monitoring accounts payable, but most organizations are still in the early stages of achieving big paybacks from Spend Management.

The Honda of America (HAM) purchasing operation is well-known for its leadership in Best Practices. The company was awarded *Purchasing* magazine's Medal of Excellence along with fellow superstars IBM, Hewlett Packard, Harley-Davidson, and Deere. As a young operation, there is much to be learned from watching Honda's growth. In the automotive industry, where lean methods first took hold in North America, this transplant operation, not unlike Toyota, has become a benchmarking trip favorite. Even Honda, however, pulls in different levels of performance for all the twenty Best Practices. Honda, for example, has always excelled at partnering and supplier development, but computer systems were not very important for planning in the early years.

Honda has always run with a good balance of numbers, a great deal of communication, and a strong end goal. In the best supply chain operations, purchasing, manufacturing, logistics, and new products work closely with each other, and may be partially combined under one executive head.

High-yield people are solutions pros, trained and paid well for taking on expanded and higher visibility work. Five years ago, less than 1 percent of all corporate boards included a chief procurement officer. Purchasing heads typically reported in to finance or manufacturing. Some boards may include an operations chief whose responsibilities include production and procurement. But until now, the purchase of raw materials and components was usually handled as a function grandfathered in by vertically integrated organizations—necessary, but not strategic. When outsourcing of parts and systems changed the amount of money spent outside, and changed the buying process as more money went outside, few corporations revised corporate boards to meet the new numbers or the new operating approach. No wonder supply chains in the 1990s continually puzzled and disappointed stockholders!

There is good news in the boardroom, however, as more supply management professionals take strategic positions at the conference table. Top procurement officers like Thomas Stallkamp, who became president of Chrysler, and Harley-Davidson's Garry Berryman combine sound purchasing techniques with executive decision-making power to deliver big value paybacks for their corporations. Good people need great systems tools, but unfortunately, purchasing systems have been slower to advance and integrate than industry needs.

Systems and Incredible Payback Technology Tools

Excellent software tools are a foundation piece of intelligent supply management. They are that extra kick that allows companies to advance from good to excellent financial returns throughout the supply chain. Software systems offer great communications, better collections, and better integration with suppliers, as well as simply good numbers describing demand and performance levels and better visibility into expensive pipelines. Ideally, customer and supplier systems display user-specified degrees of integration. Although few packages claim to meet all supply management needs, most Best Practice companies still manage to assemble a Lego-like structure of modules, user-specified information and reports, with some data gathering and analysis thrown in to guide strategic decisions and ordinary tactical operations.

We are always on the lookout for innovative software tools that, like the best-of-the-best purchasing people, enable bigger paybacks. Software tools that permit easy aggregation and monitoring of enterprise-wide performance are strategic requirements for success. However, there are few software packages that easily integrate disparate partners, and their features are typically more complicated than what is needed.

Consequently, many big customers have turned to smaller individual tools to solve specific questions. Cost analysis and cost management, tracking, product structuring and Bill of Material (B.O.M.), and Spend Management all needed to integrate procurement with other functions, especially engineering and finance. Arena Solutions, for example, a California start-up, offers manufacturing, engineering, and procurement professionals a Web-enabled tool for full B.O.M. management and data update. As an example of Web-based integrating software that brings designers and buyers together, this product life-cycle management tool is breaking new ground.

Software Solutions

Marsha Begun, former Hewlett Packard purchasing head, now a supply management consultant in Burlingame, California, believes that software solutions hold the answers to many supply chain challenges. According to Begun, the big needs for supply management systems are the ability to proactively manage risk as well as exercise strong financial controls. There is so much inventory scattered throughout the typical supply chain that it is critical to be able to manage movement and demand swings, and to do "what-ifs" on inventory positions. As tech companies know, it is quicker to ramp up factory orders than it is to shut off the machines when demand dries up. It's true for most industries that demand swings cascade instantly to increase inventory costs, and these are very difficult to track, as well as difficult to apportion to various supply chain members.

Begun tracks software developments and looks carefully at package solutions with the eye of a seasoned purchasing professional enamored of technology aids. A handful of interesting start-ups have caught her attention—Ketera, Serus, Tradec (acquired in 2003 by Agile), and Fogbreak Software—each attacking a specific set of supply chain problems, and each offering significant payback.

Ketera

Begun believes software can now solve many supply chain problems and achieve payback very quickly. "It's interesting if you talk today to lots of companies, people don't know their total spend. That's why Ketera, a California start-up backed by American Express, is having such success—their bumper sticker is 'manage spend not software.'"

Ketera is gaining traction around the following issues:

❑ *Supplier Enablement*, including online electronic catalogs transaction enablement.

❑ *The High Total Cost of Ownership*. Most companies underestimate the true total cost of ownership of Spend Management solutions. Software and maintenance fees for enterprise software solutions can reach millions in year one. Hidden costs such as supplier enablement, implementation hardware, and network services and support lines can push first-year costs even higher, all without guaranteed short-term payback.

❑ *Lack of Spend Visibility*. Spend data tends to be fragmented across many disparate systems. The data is often incomplete and not standardized into distinct, trackable categories. Most spend analysis solutions, including manual ones, are high cost and manually intensive. They take a long time to generate and they provide minimum value.

❑ *Implementation Time*. Enterprise software can take years to implement and even longer to achieve payback. Most smaller individual solutions take thirty-six months for initial implementation and results.

❑ *Resources*. Big software solutions, like MRP and ERP predecessors, require teams of experts and eager users to install. Smaller solutions, however, are quick and user-friendly; with graphic as well as data retrieval and manipulation capabilities, so they become an extension of the average buyer's day, a helpful digital servant.

Ketera offers solutions to increase spend visibility and track costs. Furthermore, the software is designed to standardize and automate routine processes, freeing up analysts for more strategic work. Kennametal illustrates how supply managers have moved from traditional procurement practices to technology innovation.

Kennametal's Incredible Payback

Latrobe, Pennsylvania, conglomerate Kennametal, owners of Cleveland Twist Drill, Diston tools, and other well-known metal-cutting equipment, searched for nearly two years for the right e-procurement solutions. Jim Cebula, Kennametal's director of global purchasing and travel purchasing and supply management, tallies up the search stats: twenty on-site visits at Latrobe, followed by forty-five teleconferences to reduce the possible solutions, and review over the Internet of seventy-five companies. And the one package they settled on was Ketera.

Kennametal's annual global spend totals nearly $700 million per year, of which travel represents just under $6 million, and total annual indirect spending (soft costs) are $390 million globally. Cebula knew there were opportunities out there, but it would take some smart tools to help uncover them.

Although Cebula's team found "a couple of software system possibilities, they just couldn't get ROI out of the seven-figure implementation costs," he recalls. Users needed to satisfy more than that one requirement, however. Kennametal wanted a one-year payback with an ROI (return on investment) that would pass internal financial requirements; but they also knew the company needed an Internet-based system that was intuitive on the level with what Cebula called an "Amazon.com training package, intuitive enough to walk through functionality by point and click. We didn't want to put a complicated purchasing tool in the hands of periodic Internet users."

The software would be used by a mix of corporate professionals, from administrative assistants to people in service operations, marketing, internal audit, and engineers supporting manufacturing. They all know exactly what they want to buy, including all the technical specs, but they were not purchasing pros skilled at negotiating terms and conditions or getting the best price. So they needed a set of simple solutions—an e-catalog of available items with predetermined prices, the speed of the Internet, and payment handled on the tail end by an American Express purchasing card.

Before Ketera, finding good numbers to leverage spend in Kennametal's decentralized procurement network was difficult and awkward. Analysts would make inquiries to the ERP systems, of which there are several, by way of the IT organizations in each business system. Kennametal has four major business units and multiple business systems, so information consolidation was difficult, but important. For instance, if someone needed to know exactly what the spend was in Europe, they would need to access four different areas, on four different platforms, and sometimes, recalls Cebula, "depending on who asked for the report, that would influence the outcome of the data!"

Paybacks

One other Kennametal system, dubbed the Purchasing Spend Cube, offered advanced spend analysis, and Cebula credits this software with helping the company to produce global analytics and get control over the spend. Kennametal's assortment of purchasing tools is called the House of Purchasing, and these combined utilities drive total cost reductions that over three years totaled $40 million. All these benefits came from what Cebula characterizes as "very low investment—in the low six figures."

The $40 million savings were generated by an assortment of analysis and management activities, including consolidation of global information, review of accounts payable, and an Internet auction. For instance, looking at their top five steel suppliers, where the spend was less than 35 percent of their dollars, Cebula felt that there was a leverage opportunity. "Kennametal," he says, "is essentially a big little company that grew from many small companies to one bigger one, so we really have to go through consolidation to leverage our spend. If we don't do that, we won't get the spend reductions." The team called for global steel quotes, and then used the Internet to conduct a global auction event, and it worked. At the same time, the government was implementing import duties and prices were rising, but Kennametal's steel prices dropped 10 percent, or $2 million, as a result of the auction. Consolidation dropped steel suppliers from five major players, to one, Latrobe Steel, a division of Timken.

Cebula believes that the ease of cost reduction was not based as much on the specific commodity as on the number of competitive suppliers of a given commodity. For example, if there are three or four qualified suppliers of a given category of spend—for example, office supplies—then, there was a good success rate in generating cost reductions. If the supplier was sole sourced, then more than likely there was not a product or service cost reduction, but internal cost savings generated by using the supplier's product or service—that is, engineered products like abrasives.

Just getting control of the information, and understanding exactly what the company's global spend is, remains a big obstacle for many traditional organizations. Jim Kindel, Kennametal's procurement specialist, who spends a lot of time worrying about systems, believes that understanding your spend—which commodities are funded from what areas—is vital, and he remains surprised about how many companies can't seem to put the numbers together and how much opportunity is there. Consultant Marsha Begun agrees, "It's interesting if you talk today to lots of companies, they do not have total visibility or understanding of their total spend. And yet reduction of total spend is their executive level mantra. That's why Ketera is having such success," and she cites a few other examples of smaller packages with "very specific, focused, and powerful solutions."

Tradec

Begun includes Tradec in her short list because their offerings provide better cost visibility for companies who outsource manufacturing. "They have unique capabilities in supply chain management . . . to make sure that users' deals with contract manufacturers are legit." Tradec enables original equipment manufacturers (OEMs), contract manufacturers (CMs), and third-party suppliers to work in synchronization. "Tools like the ones from Tradec reintroduce visibility to outsourced agreements," adds Begun.

For CMs, a big area of contention is whether the CM is passing the savings on to the OEM customer. Tradec has a platform that enables original equipment manufacturers who outsource to do a quick B.O.M. analysis, because, "and this is the key problem with outsourcing and good Spend Management, once you have outsourced things, you lose visibility to your total costs. You've lost visibility and control. All right, maybe you don't care about control because you've already outsourced the parts, and the CM is really good, but you don't want to completely lose visibility of continuing opportunities to take cost out." So Begun envisions the dialogue going something like this: "We will pay you cost plus 4 percent, so you can make your profit." There is one more step, however. With cost management software, the OEM does the analysis of what the product costs. It's a challenge to really understand the total cost and then the challenge is increased exponentially once the product is outsourced.

Customers must have an up-to-date Bill of Material to start constructing the cost models. Tradec's B.O.M. analysis offers purchasers a tool to help continually drive costs down by adding up and maintaining every bit of cost data to the master file. Begun advises users to "take a holistic approach—from idea phase to obsolescence—in your cost modeling. Its not just what's the cost of a capacitor or the cost of a PC board, people have pretty good cost models on what a PC board or a dram should cost. The analysis leads to other questions like 'What should it cost by volume?'" Maybe the buyer should be looking to pay by unit, per product, per truckload, per ocean container. All these factors have to go into the cost model, and the one-time engineering tooling cost, labor, all the nonmaterial costs as well. The cost-model factors are not new, but typically this type of analysis is performed with Excel spreadsheets. This type of manual process consumes massive amounts of time and human resources. Begun contends that purchasers need software applications that can work well and integrate continuously to other applications, ensuring ongoing, real-time analyses.

Serus

Another technology solutions provider that Begun is watching is Serus of Mountainview, California, an enterprise software solutions provider. Serus addresses the problem of product management and delivery to customers with fulfillment problems, such as the wrong product, wrong dates, or geographical limitations.

According to Begun, Serus software allows buyers to "real-time, anytime, figure out where inventory is at any stage. If, for example, you have inventory that is classified as work in process, but you haven't yet configured it—kind of like Dell's 'have it your way' model—it will be useful to know up to the time of configuration that it could be configured in X, Y, Z flavors. This software solution allows planners to create a product mix probability scenario, and then make optimal decisions driven by financial, marketing, or other specific initiatives."

Mix Management, Pipeline Visibility

The software enables product allocation to satisfy best financial, or marketing, or building impact. It's a simple process. First, identify the most profitable orders. "If I have one order from Joe, who buys millions of dollars worth of equipment from me every year, and only one order from Dave, and if I know that Joe always buys the supertech high-end chip, and I only have enough boxes to complete one unit for either him or Dave, then of course the unit will be sold to Joe! Presto, this software allows mix to be managed inside the pipelines." Says Begun, "Finance and operations love this, but purchasing is new to it all." And the software provides real-time product availability and commit dates. This is a revolutionary inroad for purchasing, planning, and sales to exploit profitability opportunities.

It also provides real-time product availability and commit dates relative to different component or product scenarios. Substitutions take on real purpose and payback.

Inventory and Order Management Are Commodity Trading!

Think of the scheduling and inventory investment possibilities. Says Begun, "The software can assess component or product scenarios. For example, if Joe once took lime green or yellow units, but Gene wants only purple, the software allows substitution scenarios. Inventory replenishment can be done at multiple locations and levels of the Bill of Material. The decision to use a specific color happens at the molders, for instance, so if buyers know what is going on at their plastic injection molders, they can figure out the trade-offs. And when customer orders become more complex, like when a new customer, Jones, wants a bunch of units shipped all over the world, software provides answers. Jones won't want us to ship a unit out of Michigan to his niece in Bali, for example, so software enables us to ask if we have any purple units sitting in Singapore."

Serus allows supply chain mangers to reconcile their inventory in different sales channels. For example, if there are dozens of purple units in the sales channels, and people in Michigan are scrambling for purple, software provides the visibility and the choice of directing purple product to Michigan.

Furthermore, the software should identify price elasticity of the product to allow trade-offs. If prices in Singapore are more elastic than they are in Michigan, planners can decide and forecast how much each finished unit will earn by where it is being shipped. The software offers users a unique combination of planning, execution, and resolution functions—solve the problem and ship the product! It marries inventory planning to execution in units, with the corresponding financial analysis to solve bad service/bad financial decision problems. A company does not want to ship 500 units for $500 to New Hampshire, for instance, if they can instead go to Michigan for $1,000. The important capability technology offers supply chain is the ability to analyze product financials all the time, the same way a commodity trader manages her soybean or orange juice orders.

Serus was founded in 2000 by Indu Bingham, an engineer who learned at an early age the real problems of dispatching and moving materials. Bingham worked in her father's dairy back in India, where she proved herself a whiz kid, calculating complicated truck dispatch schedules, in her head, at age five! Along the way, she learned first-hand the difficulties of balancing profitability against inventories in a complex supply chain.

Reconciliation of sales orders against pipeline and in-process inventory saves shipping costs and makes customers very happy, since it offers companies the opportunity to maximize profits of pipeline sales. "Serus offers a unique combination," says Begun, "of planning, execution, and resolution functions—solve the problem and ship the product. Marry inventory planning to execution with the corresponding financial analysis. Supply chain managers need to analyze their product financials all the time."

Recovering the Lost Possibilities

Bingham echoes Begun's analogy: "We help manufacturing companies understand what their financial liability is in their supply chain. Every decision has a financial implication—whether it is expediting orders or building more raw material—there is financial exposure with every move." It's difficult to calculate the best way to fulfill customer orders, but to raise profitability and meet revenue goals, planners need to be able to identify where and how their product can bring in the most cash. In the global supply chain, every non-value cost counts, from expediting to supporting fabrication in China or assembly in Taiwan. Fast-track manufacturing, for example, a premium service provided with shorter delivery quotes from contract manufacturers, adds cost.

Bingham's software solution lets manufacturers dollarize their different options and helps them to understand what the negotiated contract was and what it actually costs. "People have not been able to understand their true costs—they get an invoice and just pay it. We say it's all valuable lost information. We have to get away from being reactionary. When the problem happens, people run around to solve it. We are helping producers be more proactive, because the cost to be reactive is ten times higher," says Bingham.

Serus's customer base includes companies that reflect Bingham's drive to lower pipeline costs in complex networks—Cisco; Quantum Corporation, a new telecom founded by executives at Lucent; ISSI; Binc; Flash Electronics; and BMK Inc., the nation's largest distributor of nonfood items to grocery stores and retail stores. Serus helps them make hundreds of decisions daily about inventory pipeline costs: where to place it and how to respond when the price varies. One customer that buys from Procter and Gamble and Revlon is learning to manage the relationship between suppliers and manufacturing and grocery stores. "As the margins are dropping," warns Bingham, "this is crucial to avoid waste." The software starts by capturing basic data from the current ERP system—on-hand inventory and sales orders, and the purchase orders released to suppliers—and provides analytical tools to use the numbers well.

Serus's Payback

The cost to get started is about $100,000 to $250,000, with payback in about three to four months' time, including the first two months ramp-up operating at about 50 percent efficiency. Like many of the other software solution ideas that we believe will bring better technology tools to the supply chain, this collaboration and optimization solution is not a massive investment and it has a solid payback. Bingham points to the huge opportunities ahead in this growing market; her two-year-old company focused on customer acquisition from day one, and refused venture capital offers in favor of hard orders plus a little angel investment funding, and the payback for Serus has been doubled revenues in less than one year, a pretty happy return.

Fogbreak, the Beginnings

In 1985 a Vietnamese teenager named Trung Dung finally cleared the wait list and left the Indonesian refugee camp that he had called home for a year. Trung, whose family remained back in Vietnam, used those endless twelve months of waiting and dreaming to learn English. "My written skills are better than speaking," he says, as he launches into a passionate explanation of why domain experts and technologists, like himself, are the future of supply chain.

Trung's travels landed him, still without family, in a tripledecker apartment in blue-collar Dorchester, Massachusetts, a mixed community from which thousands of Irish, then Jewish, Asian, Haitian, and African-American immigrants have made their way. Trung was in a hurry—he needed a college degree and a master's degree too, because he had to get going and found companies, three at least. But his college counselor stopped him short with the news that he would first need a high-school degree, because his formal education in Vietnam had ended in his junior year of high school before he could apply to college. Not one to be delayed by serial processing of his educational plan, Dung intended to do everything in parallel, including an undergraduate computer science degree and his GED, so he dug in.

One master's degree and three companies later, Trung believes he has created a powerful nexus of domain expertise and technology that can take supply chain management to a rich new level of planning and control. Trung was an early technical contributor at Open Market, the first developer of Internet commerce software; that experience led him to found OnDisplay, Inc., a pioneering developer of e-business infrastructure products. As founder and CEO of Fogbreak, Trung has cleared an obstacle that blocked supply chain advances for many years. According to Trung, "You have technology people trying to design supply chain software, but we need to be able to combine, and it's a very difficult thing, the software world with deep domain expertise, because it's the only way to design the right software." Dung believes that users with domain expertise have had too little say in software development. "If you look at the landscape, you'll see some very strong technologies, and very often they are technology solutions looking for a problem! Or there are deep domain people with shallow technology expertise. We haven't had a good mix." Dung teamed up with IBM, Quantum, and Gateway Computer supply chain veteran Jim Booth to be sure both sides of the challenge—technology and domain expertise—were recognized.

Booth believes access to basics, such as the B.O.M. coupled with data from ERP systems, are key to integrating sophisticated software in supply chain operations. "Many people don't look at the B.O.M. in a lot [of] different simple ways that would help them decide what type of actions to take to improve performance."

Booth cites their work with an OEM and contract manufacturer that supplies Automated Teller Machine (ATM) producers with printed circuit assemblies. The OEM had a very unhappy customer who was tired of long nine-week lead-time quotes; four weeks was what they wanted, not at all an impossible dream, they thought. But for the supplier, meeting a four-week lead-time was "not just shaving the lead-time a little here and there, it was a 50 percent cut," said Booth.

The OEM and CM tried to do it, however, struggling the traditional way by looking at the longest lead-time items in the B.O.M., and recalls Booth, "beating up suppliers." Fogbreak, however, takes a different approach that allows producers to put resources where they will have the most and smartest impact.

Bill of Material Profiling

What if users could value their Bill of Material and learn which items weighed in with the most value in the B.O.M.? Profiling the bill structure allows users to understand where the costs appear in time. When Fogbreak plotted the contract manufacturer's B.O.M., the company was surprised to learn that 2 percent of the value of the B.O.M. appeared in weeks nine to thirteen, and then between six to nine weeks was 40 percent of the B.O.M. cost. It's a revealing exercise that gives users a feeling for what the real problems are, and what they actually cost. Plus, says Booth, "It helps you make a decision about where to put the effort. If only 2 percent is beyond nine weeks, you could have an inventory strategy—carry inventory to compensate, instead of the tail wagging the dog. Even though the problem item may be the longest lead time, it may be very solvable. So then you find out there are other parts, like raw boards that are in the 40 percent value, six-week range. Wow, you only have to improve one week for it not to be a problem! It's almost embarrassingly simple, from a domain perspective! Then if you look at 25 percent of the value of the bill for the CM—it could be a chip set and processors—the software has pointed to your next supplier discussion."

So, the software becomes a problem-identification tool that shows users where their money is accumulating in the profile. In the chip world, where buyers wait in line for scarce items—no cutting in the queue—understanding well in advance that a particular commodity requires a really good sourcing strategy is worth millions. It's not enough to simply look at the lead time—users will want to decide whether to gear up their distribution or inventory sourcing strategies.

Booth explains that profiling raises a whole new set of questions about sourcing, "How do I look at it? Because looking at a part by itself is not enough, that part is now a valuable commodity. I have to look at it and decide, when I see the entire company, what is my entire spend with my supplier, what are the parts, what's their commonality, where are they in my supplier's product set, could I inventory them through distribution, or the CM's inventory?" The software will drive creation of independent strategies, and at the end, users should have five or six choices that will make a big financial and service improvement.

Back to our original customer lead-time problem. With the OEM and CM, Fogbreak was able to reduce the lead time below six weeks, approaching four. "The bottom line," said Booth, was that "because they had done the profiling work, they knew where to focus their efforts with significant results." Users extracted data from ERP—the usual B.O.M., lead time, and cost data at the component level, generated a file, and let the software grind away. Next, the OEM supplied an Excel file of all their commodity lead times from standard commodity strategies. Planners then plotted exactly what came out of ERP, comparing strategic items as negotiated with suppliers, and they discovered that the negotiated items did not always match what the system said. "And that," says Booth, "is the real problem with what has been negotiated. Nobody integrates, or has a repository for critical data showing commodity managers what the buyers are actually executing against. We provide them that form of comparison."

What comes next is pure execution to new targets because once the gaps between negotiated and operating facts are clear, planners can set targets, by customer or situation. For every big gap, there's a new discussion and a better strategy. In the OEM-CM example, for instance, users wanted to do analysis by commodity, and when they learned that certain components showed 70 percent forecast accuracy, they asked themselves, recalls Booth, "Why am I not running much more risk on these parts. I can go to subcontractors, and ask them with very high forecast-to-consumption accuracy to carry some parts in inventory. In fact," he emphasizes, "I can guarantee you that we will buy one week's supply and have effective reduction in lead time. The manufacturer in our example was able to convince their CM to put one week's inventory aside, and pull everything else in. Bingo! All of a sudden, what appeared as a massive problem went away. They had to fix a few delayed components for which commodity managers had negotiated two-week lead times, but with the standard ERP lead time at eight weeks, in this case they were able to go to a subcontractor and renegotiate the eight weeks quote down to two. In fact, *92 percent of the Bill of Material moved into lower lead times.* We closed the gap between what commodity managers had negotiated and what planners were working with."

Payback

So what's the payback in real dollars? The users saved millions—and turned around a very unhappy customer—from an investment of a couple hundred thousand. Plus, buyers experienced no cost increases in their other products while they reduced risk.

"This tool fills a big supply management system gap," says Booth, "because it replaces back-of-envelope calculations that are not integrated with ERP or supplier contracts. For users, it's pure fun to tweak and do what-if analyses—*if* they have the data!"

Software can solve the reconciliation war as well. When contract manufacturers are hit with big changes from customers, the battle rages over who agreed to what, exactly what prices and clauses were negotiated, and who eats the excess inventory. Traditionally, the argument centers on forecast changes, but producers could just as well throw pipeline inventory into the battle—if they could figure out exactly what's left out there. It's an unhealthy process that creates animosity and distrust.

But what if buyers could articulate the details of their agreements, all the flex-up, and flex-down calculations? With good pipeline management software, planners can tell customers and suppliers exactly what they own and where it is in the pipeline. The lines of financial responsibility become very clear, very quickly, when the numbers are there. "In fact," says Trung, "we can time stamp what you did and where, and what it did to the financials. Here's what your planner changed last week—here's the part and here's what it cost, and we can even produce a money-phased MRP action report telling planners what it costs to cancel capacitors, for example, within thirty days of shipment. Or we can time-phase the action reports to be sure you know within your financial liability period that there is a part hitting excess inventory limits!" Now that takes a lot of the punch out of the argument over who eats what! But without the numbers, it's hard to turn down the invoice.

Next up for this type of software innovation is "tying it all together," says Trung. The ERP data and everything else companies currently work with, especially the information stored in the agreement translated from legalese to numbers that describe flexibility, liability, buffer stocks, flex-up, and flex-down. Developers are putting these terms all together into a rich library of terms. It's the beginning of a new body of knowledge with Incredible Payback.

With the terms and numbers defined, developers can apply a simple algorithm to calculate buys based on forecasts, history, and variance parameters. The breakthrough comes with being able to combine ERP snapshots of the current situation with forecast and contract data, and display it in an easy graphical format that allows buyers and planners to see the strategic impact of changes they request.

When Trung Dung left OnDisplay, his previous start-up, he wanted to build a new company that had guaranteed payback on the applications side. The concept had to start somewhere with available data, and it seemed to him that starting with the information contained in the contract, the data that "nobody owns," would go to the heart and soul of every partnership, which is the agreement. "But what happens," Trung asked himself, "if that agreement is stuck in the drawer and we have day-to-day people executing with no idea about the inherent misalignment between tactical execution and the strategy? I used the agreement as the starting point, but I didn't have domain expertise, although I knew it was a pretty good general purpose idea, so I hooked up with Jim early on and talked with a lot of people and was able to identify the key problem, the issue of supply chain liability." Other cost factors can be added to the strategic contract numbers, including warranty service and repair, even promotions and rebates.

Fogbreak aims to be a leader in the next generation of enterprise solutions by helping supply chain managers deal with risk and the financial costs of guessing wrong. The idea is to enable companies to anticipate, track, and manage the costs associated with building and delivering products in an environment of demand uncertainty. Improving manufacturers' financial performance by tightly aligning direct material execution with Best

Practice strategies helps to balance customer expectations, inventory risks, outsourcing partners, and supplier performance.

Complex supply chains with numerous suppliers and customers show too much demand and service variation to be well managed without computer assists. Furthermore, financial exposure to excess and obsolete inventory can derail the best financials and the best commodity strategies. One way to quantify and track exposure and liability with customers and suppliers is to maintain visibility to critical components and identify at-risk components and possible mitigation actions.

One leading semiconductor capital equipment company uses Fogbreak to manage direct materials execution with its contract manufacturers and suppliers. Another premier electronics contract manufacturer (ECM) uses Fogbreak to manage liability with its OEM customers and component suppliers. Other customers have discovered that Fogbreak will help them maintain greater visibility to account for widely disbursed assets, such as inventory, an ability that will become more crucial as government regulations demand more accurate accounting.

Sarbanes-Oxley Act

The Enron scandals sparked demand for better accounting for inventory transactions, as well as off-balance sheet assets and income. The federal Sarbanes-Oxley Act specifically mandates in Section 401(a) disclosure requirements of off-balance sheet transactions and other agreements that may have material effect on the financial performance and statements of a company. For supply managers, this means they must track pockets of information throughout their supply chains for items that fall under the act's definition but were never part of a balance sheet or a financial report in the past. Many components of sourcing and supply chain execution will now need to be tracked, evaluated for total financial impact, and included in public disclosure, including:

- ❏ Purchasing commitments toward material
- ❏ Actual material assets acquired by the supplier on the company's behalf
- ❏ User or pay capacity arrangements
- ❏ Minimum volume guarantees to vendors
- ❏ Contractual commitments to forecast and order

Again, software may offer a workable solution for these new requirements, and Fogbreak is one of the products that is pioneering this area. The Sarbanes-Oxley requirements may force management to find ways to integrate the contractual terms and supply chain visibility across multiple layers on the buy side and the sell side.

The Spreadsheet Solution

Consultant Marsha Begun believes that most OEMs and CMs are addicted to spreadsheets that gather data and try out different financial outcomes. Even inside a single company, different spreadsheet versions exist. "I've got mine and the CFO has his, and the supplier has his. How can we put these different views together so that my boss sees the same message?" she asks.

The answer is supply management software, in small doses, and it is available for those who want to look. Begun's consulting base includes ongoing and watchful analysis of software offerings, and she feels that big is not necessarily the answer. A proliferation of various spreadsheets isn't the final solution either. Although there were hundreds more small software tool solutions before the dot.com implosion that took many good ones off the market, Begun believes good and valuable software packages are still available. And for many companies, smaller is indeed much better—new product preparation and launch, for example, is quicker and cheaper with powerful software design and tracking tools.

Beware Behemoths

OEMs and contract manufacturers in electronics have all learned that a "muscular hunk with no fine motor skills," Begun's apt description of software behemoths, means that they are not flexible or rich enough to offer workable real-time operating analysis. Begun warns against sellers who pitch big packages as "do-all, be-alls." According to Begun, "Big packages do a whole lot of things, but they aren't everything to everyone in the enterprise. If they were, companies would not be managing major complex initiatives and strategies off of spreadsheets." Furthermore, with the trend toward increased outsourcing, the puzzle just gets crazier and cloudier because OEMs operate one way, the CMs another, and their systems don't easily integrate or collaborate in terms of data sharing.

The original impetus to outsource based on careful assessment of core competencies remains viable. But out of those complex analyses came new problems, a major one being lack of visibility in the outsourced supply chain, thereby complicating the inventory and customer fulfillment objectives. If OEMs lose clear visibility into the supply chain and material pipeline, they cannot effectively gauge their exposure, and that hurts. Companies like Cisco and others have suffered big losses from supply chain surprises. Everyone, even giants like Cisco, needs clearer and longer line of sight to the pipeline.

"OEMs," says Begun, "need to see their inventory, their WIP, their exposure every day. Some CMs will say, 'But you don't need visibility! We've got you covered!'" but Begun sees a growing philosophical chasm between CMs and OEMs. "OEMs have an almost paternalistic view—'I control you and you'll do what I want'— that's not really correct. Although the CM may salute and respond 'Yes, sir,' they really consider themselves sovereign, reporting only to themselves and their shareholders, by no means an extension of the OEM. This is a serious mismatch. An equitable relationship is needed. With CMs significantly and quickly expanding their role in the supply chain, through acquisition and positioning, both sides need to come to the table on this, each recognizing the other's leverage points."

Finding the Money

There is simply too much cash at play in inventories throughout the pipelines for good financial software tools not to be in constant use. Spend Management, for example, is best achieved with excellent and fast software tools. We mentioned Ketera as an example of an analysis tool that allows buyers to look quickly at spending from different angles. It's important to remember that although visibility toward total spend should be easily available, most spend analysis solutions are high cost and manually intensive. They take a long time to complete, and they often must be repeated, from scratch, when updates are needed. Therefore, companies tend to underestimate the time and resources required to produce base Spend Management data.

The second barrier to comprehensive Spend Management for many enterprise partners is the problem that so many suppliers lack good electronic transaction information, such as catalog (price, specs, etc.) management, transaction enablement, and project management. Without these three electronic capabilities, customers will continue to be frustrated when they try to accomplish basic Spend Management tasks. It will continue to be difficult for customers to roll supplier data into their spend plans.

Performance Tracking and Supplier Evaluation

Supplier evaluation and performance forecasting present another big challenge for the extended enterprise. Although suppliers complain of endless audits and different quality systems requirements for different customers, a few innovative solutions are available that capitalize on the fact that much of the data that customers require of suppliers is available in various sources and it can be summarized to tell a coherent story. Lori Frantzve's Intellimet start-up and Sherry Gordon's Valuedge both offer software solutions designed to take the guesswork out of supplier evaluation. The technology of Intellimet in today's post–9-11 environment has the ability to identify criticality and vulnerability in the supply chain. The software is positioned to look at material flow interruptions, and it captures all the variables to determine the vulnerability of that supplier. For one high-tech company, Intellimet identified the material processes and the components for their semiconductor supply chain, which allowed the customer to plan for risk mitigation.

Not all good systems are digital, however, especially in the world of manufacturing and material movement. We said that building The Incredible Payback organization requires smart technology tools, as well as good basic flow systems. A descendant of both the Toyota and Honda Production systems, Delphi's Manufacturing System had won the company twenty Shingo awards by 2004, but this system wasn't digital. Good supplier development and lean manufacturing systems throughout the enterprise have won Incredible Payback for Delphi. In fact, most of the Toyota Production System and the Delphi Manufacturing System is supported by manual *kanbans* and *heijunka* (scheduling) boards.

Manufacturing Systems for Big Payback

Tools to improve manufacturing performance—kaizen, just-in-time, 2P/3P,[2] Web-enabled scheduling, and B.O.M. systems—contribute to waste reduction in manufacturing processes. They can be used in white-collar operations such as order administration as well, but essentially these Japanese processes clarify the process. Although they may yield big paybacks, easily 20 to 50 percent savings in inventory, cycle time, space, and quality rejects, some companies never get all their processes, all their work centers, online—it's a big challenge that involves more than technical changes. Simple systems seem to be most effective in manufacturing operations where problems like long cycle times and inventory waste clog pull systems.

The Delphi Manufacturing System is a wonderful second-generation tool that increases productivity for Delphi and its suppliers as well. Companies like Delphi that learn from the best and design their own custom manufacturing and sourcing methods from studying Honda and Toyota are filled with energy and hope. It makes sense to adapt the standard Honda/Toyota system components to their particular challenge and to place emphasis where the work most needs to be done. A great manufacturing system isn't enough to consistently deliver the big payback, but it's a good starting place.

Let's take a look at how one leader went about creating an innovative operation from scratch in less than five years. This young operation combined Best Practices, well-trained young professionals, a strong overriding philosophy, supplier development, and some technology tools, to become the best of the best.

Putting It All Together—People, Training, Systems, and Rewards to Build Honda's North American Capabilities

The growth of Honda's North American operations illustrates solid development in purchasing, as well as some innovative approaches not found in most nontransplant operations. The Honda model proves how companies can grow and morph in a short time when purchasing leverages strategies. By the late 1980s, Honda's Ohio assembly operations were supported by 45 percent localization of components and assemblies used in Honda's cars and motorcycles. Local suppliers provided steel parts, seats, and tire assemblies. Still, although other commodities continued to arrive from Japan, plans were in place to move some supplier operations from Japan to North America, or to place orders with local suppliers as soon as they could be qualified.

Identifying and developing partnerships with local suppliers was hard work. Honda purchasing managers identified parts that were candidates for localization; next planners hit the road to visit and review American suppliers. Although they found some pretty good capabilities, for many of the more sophisticated parts in which buyers would have liked to use American suppliers—fuel injectors, for instance—Honda was forced to rely on offshore sources.

The story of how purchasing decided to locally source engine control units (ECUs), a small computer that runs engine timing and fuel functions, illustrates the challenge to localize with excellent North American versus Japanese suppliers.

One day, the Honda manager in charge of electronics stopped into his purchasing manager's office with some bad news. It seems that a Motorola vice president had been called and asked to move his unit price from an original quote by about 15 percent to about the same level that Honda's internal Indianapolis supplier was quoting to meet Honda's target cost. Although Honda buyers expected this request would be routinely met after some careful forecast and pricing discussions, they were turned down.

A friend overheard the phone call, a manager who had at one time led Motorola's sales and marketing, and his feedback was stunning. He quietly offered to share a bit of advice. "You've got to do something here a little different," he explained. "I know the whole situation, and what you are asking that man to do, he does not have the authority to decide, and if he did, he would eventually get fired. Quoting $124 would have put that business in there at a loss. Now, I don't mean to tell you how to do your business, but truly, there is only one guy who can do it—and he would make the decision in an instant. His name is Chris Galvin, and he's the president."

With this insightful advice, Honda's purchasing department

set up a meeting for the next morning to gather everyone together and prepare in advance of the big meeting with Mr. Galvin. Despite the early hour, everyone showed up—sales, the account manager, and some marketing vice presidents. No one was happy to be ignored, and various justifications for the higher price flew by. Of course, escalating this type of decision to the president was not a popular action, as well, and the early morning crowd let the Honda executive know it.

Within about five minutes, it became clear that the meeting was veering off-track, taking with it the potential for new business. Politically, it was a delicate problem, but strategically, the problem of cementing a long-term relationship with a top-tier U.S. supplier was even more critical. Honda management scrambled to explain that this was not an end-run, unusual circumstances that called for unusual methods, it's all for the greater good, and so forth. Motorola reps listened, and the air lightened up as early morning coffee warmed the room, creating a more convivial atmosphere. By 8 A.M., after an honest and frank disclosure of Honda's need to localize, they were ready for the next step, a decision from Mr. Galvin.

The partnering and financial reasons were clear: Honda wanted to buy the new ECU from Motorola because they were a true-blue, local, U.S. supplier with great capabilities in ECU technology. The transplant's growing product offerings included four- and six-cylinder engines for the Marysville and Anna, Ohio, plants. Although these plants had originally depended on an Indianapolis source and a Japanese supplier, as the company became more established, the Honda strategy was to design and build vehicles in the markets they served. Honda was preparing to launch its first high-end American sedan, which was designed and built by Americans for Americans, and now that the company was established with an American engine plant, it only made sense to find an American ECU supplier as well.

Quite a dilemma. Honda wanted as many American parts as

purchasing could find or develop, and the opportunity to form a partnership with Motorola was very attractive. Although Honda knew it could make the unit for less than its Indianapolis plant, a small facility designed and run by the Japanese, the company had decided it would pay three or four dollars more to buy from Motorola.

It didn't take Mr. Galvin fifteen minutes to see the strategic opportunity and to decide: "You don't have to pay our entry into this market, we want it really bad," recalls coauthor Nelson. Galvin felt the company could afford to make the ECU at a loss for a little while, until they got it done right. Motorola would invest in the equipment and tooling, and eventually the price would come down to a point close to the transplant supplier's and truly achieve Honda's target cost.

Many parts and commodities were brought into North America and sourced locally over just this type of negotiation, a focused give-and-take that addressed strategic supply base development, and ramping up supplier capabilities as prices were reduced. In most cases, although Honda had various Japanese supplier options, the company's preference for local parts drove its sourcing strategies to try out new solutions.

It was a strategy that did not always work as planned. Some U.S. suppliers over the years had become accustomed, for example, to missing their Detroit automotive customers' launch dates. But when they began to supply transplants, to keep the business these suppliers had to learn The Honda Way because it was important to never, ever miss a launch. These companies, of necessity, acquired new project management skills, as well as just-in-time expertise. Crisis management declined and everyday attention to detail became a practiced skill in good North American competitors.

The groundbreaking Honda-Motorola partnership pointed the way toward many more successful local deals. Clearly, this type of detailed cost management data is key to Spend Management paybacks. Good relationships are built on trust as well as honest and accurate data, the kind that open-book accounting proponents are famous for. The methods companies like Toyota and Honda use to plan and control parts cost—down to the penny—keep them in top market positions. It's their rigorous and systematic approach to planning and achieving targeted retail prices that is enabled by solid cost management expertise.

Cost Management Drives Price and Production Strategies

Cost tables and cost management—the way companies like Honda and Toyota do it—are a critical and objective approach to negotiated partnerships that will be new to many companies. The approach requires developing a best cost, or detailed breakdown listing of exactly what a cost should be for a particular part or assembly, down to the raw material, labor, and other value-added processes. The best cost becomes a target toward which a supplier works. If the part is a new one, a target cost drives the entire cascading price structure of a new part. The Japanese are particularly skilled customers who understand the technology and price elements of most suppliers' costs, sometimes better than suppliers do themselves.

Using a calculated cost forces many issues, and it makes payback clearer. Customers and suppliers must work together to review detailed costs; they need to understand new directions coming up in technology and raw materials. When cost drives a product's design as well as the sourcing plan, the bar goes up a few notches for more competitive performance on both sides.

The key word is *competitive*. When transplant companies and those who have mastered cost management build detailed cost models, they are able to approach purchasing in a totally different way. The emphasis shifts to quantitative analysis, rather than leverage and heavy-handed negotiations. A Japanese customer, for instance, will not squeeze a U.S. supplier to sell parts cheaper than they could buy them from a Japanese transplant. Instead, when customers know exactly what the target cost should be, they force competitive pricing that raises the bar on performance. The traditional "Lopez" approach—breaking contracts and forcing price reductions without a plan to reduce actual costs—often seen among U.S. companies, costs suppliers profits and health. Cost management installed in a competitive operation is not designed to bankrupt suppliers, but to improve their competitive position by forcing non-value-added waste out of the operation. Every component, every production operation, each time the part is moved or touched, is subject to expert review. That's how suppliers to Honda and Toyota eliminate waste, remove cost, and share price reductions.

So, an important tool for high payback enterprises is good cost management. Delphi has begun an intensive project to build cost standards as good as those used by Honda and Toyota. Their starting point, a veteran Toyota purchasing cost expert, Mr. Kamimura, has contributed the methods upon which the company will continue to build expertise around all contributors to cost. This is traditional cost accounting in Japan, with detailed accumulation of actual breakdowns from parts—kilograms of steel, minutes of labor, and cost of machine and tooling for every operation as well as production schedules. The more complete the breakdown, the easier it is to build and maintain good cost standards.

Cost standards were one of the first supply management capabilities that purchasing at Honda of America implemented based on their Japanese roots. Cost standards helped the new operation to develop purchasing expertise, and formed the trust and openness around which customer and supplier cost discussions centered.

How Did They Do It?

Although the HAM Marysville and Anna, Ohio, auto complex was not immediately independent, over a one- to two-year period it developed great internal capabilities and installed mostly local talent. The growth of HAM's purchasing function paralleled growth in the supply base. In 1989, the organization's three hundred purchasing pros supported three hundred suppliers; by the early 1990s, four hundred planners and buyers supported an equal number of suppliers.

Honda's strategy was to build and expand in local markets, most of which happened to offer lower manufacturing costs than Japan. Delphi is taking a similar approach to structuring its global supply chain, building a stronger presence in lower cost countries where it does business. Like Honda's growth strategy of putting purchasing into a new country well in advance of production, Delphi believes that it can improve payback more quickly by moving purchasing intelligence into more low-cost countries. Delphi has learned that moving into lower cost countries builds agility; it helps to leverage the spend and make the enterprise more responsive to global market shifts.

Recently, Delphi was able to generate incredible opportunities in a relatively short time by hiring sixty-eight purchasing people in low-cost countries to support their customers in these regions. These experts will identify, qualify, and source local suppliers. They will develop detailed cost models to guide product development. Then, suppliers will join up with engineering centers that are already in place.

Expanding and Consolidating

This expansion strategy complements the movement of Delphi to combine engineering, manufacturing, and purchasing responsibilities under Donald Runkle, vice chairman of enterprise technologies, and to localize engineering expertise. Engineering centers positioned close to new, emerging customers incorporate local market needs. It is a requirement of top customers like Toyota that suppliers be close to their design centers to ensure fast and accurate communication throughout the design and development process.

Customers like Mercedes, for instance, find it too confusing to deal with six different sites for an assortment of supplier projects. Innovators are taking their lead from Toyota, whose Tochigi complex north of Tokyo is where all Toyotas are designed and engineered, and from Honda, where cars destined for North American consumers were designed in North America starting about seven years ago with the Acura CL.

The Role of Sensei

Amazingly, although a typical Honda growth plan puts purchasing into a country in advance of manufacturing, this is not the traditional sequence. Such an innovative plan guarantees that when production starts up, there are fewer supply glitches and more local suppliers ready to meet the assembly plants' just-in-time demands. Japanese sensei like Teruyuki Maruo, the father of the Honda Production System called BP (Best Position, Best Productivity Partner, Best Product, Best Price, Best Partners) came on board when North American operations started, and stayed until he determined that the U.S. workforce had achieved the same basic skills as the Japanese team members. He is credited with being the philosophical "glue" and teacher that started the Marysville complex.

Maruo needed to know in particular that North American purchasing people could work with suppliers The Honda Way, a philosophy-based approach to doing business. It was important for them to understand how to form long-term partnering relationships, and how to see a factory, whether it was their own or the supplier's, the way the Japanese would. Every company runs to a formal mission statement, supported with unstated philosophies and procedures, and colored by legends and myths. Honda's basic strategy, starting over fifty years ago with the founder's collaboration with motorcycle suppliers to crack the automotive market, extending down through the company's sixth decade of growth, has been to focus on and hold to the philosophy behind its operations.

That umbrella philosophy expresses the company's overall principles, and in many ways it dictates how to treat people—employees and suppliers alike.

The Honda Way expresses to employees inside the company, and to suppliers and customers on the outside, how the company does business, what approaches to business relationships are the preferred mode of operation, and how to make day-to-day operating decisions that reflect the company's best objectives. This philosophy guides associates' everyday actions and decision making, as well as the way associates treat relationships; respect for the individual is the foundation for this philosophy. Soichiro Honda was a blunt and direct innovator who respected real knowledge and loyalty, and his legacy lives in the character of Honda's work environment. Associates come to understand that his umbrella-like philosophy helps clarify decisions and good results, like the Three Joys.

One of The Honda Way's tenets is that work affords an opportunity to experience the Three Joys. The first joy is the joy of making a high-quality product, the second joy is selling a high-quality and efficient product, and the third joy is buying a good product. Suppliers participate in the execution of these philosophies because they understand that they are building Accords and Civics—not parts and not components.

Respect for the individual is at the foundation, but truly, sensei Maruo's objective was to teach purchasing people how to create those relationships from the very beginning. This artful skill became a kind of joint effort, one in which Maruo let the Americans take the lead with U.S. suppliers. His intent was to let American customer/supplier partnerships deepen to all levels of the organization, until other functions like engineering, manufacturing, and service management bought in. He knew that getting everyone on board meant they had to agree philosophically, which was the real challenge. Doing purchasing and partnering The Honda Way represented a new philosophy for North Americans.

The Honda Way guaranteed, of course, that trainees would learn the basics, just as they did in Japan. In Japan, a college graduate who is a new hire is not expected to demonstrate great job expertise immediately. To the sensei, a college diploma quite simply meant that an employee had the capability to complete college. It really did not matter, however, what kind of degree the new hire brought with him, other than a U.S. preference for diplomas from the better purchasing schools, because the first five years or so at Honda would be spent learning other more valuable skills, like project management.

Project Management the A-3 Way

First off, all new Honda hires learn a special method of job management, a prerequisite used every day in a variety of ways. It's Honda's approach to planning and executing all work, and the A-3 describes in workable detail various operating tasks such as how to work with a group of people to outline and monitor a new project. Trainees learn that they must write on a chart everything that is being agreed to. If the task at hand is an engineering issue, the A-3 is a method of capturing everything on that one chart. As the discussion moves on, no task is forgotten, and there is agreement at each step. At the conclusion, copies are distributed to every attendee, and it's on to the next challenge.

At Honda, every meeting room, conference room, and work area is equipped with a photocopying white board. The A-3 chart allows team members to boil each bit of project work to a single page; although it may be more difficult and takes more time to compress an entire meeting onto one sheet of paper, the process is powerful and facilitates good execution, a skill Honda is renowned for. Furthermore, the single page sharpens focus and forces agreement on key issues. Every A-3 covers seven areas—high-level strategy, method and approach, current process, high-level objectives, planning targets, process description, and timeline (see Figure

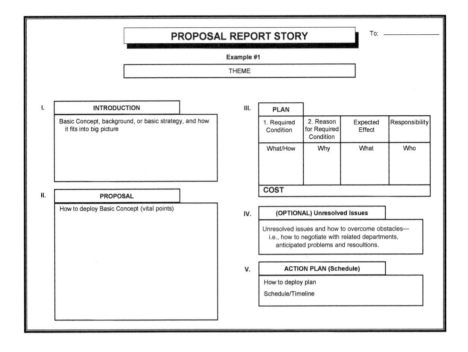

Figure 5–1. A–3 template.

5–1). The same A-3 format applies whether the team member is from purchasing or engineering.

The A-3 assigns responsibilities and dates to specific team members and makes it easy to sum up project progress. For example, when a buyer meets with a supplier, although the buyer may be working with many sheets of paper, a single A-3 will be made from it. In a meeting to set quality levels, for instance, the engineers will contribute their input on specifications, as well as that of the buyers', but the final agreement on exactly what those quality parameters are must appear in the A-3. Later discussions about who agreed to what are eliminated when attendees pull out their A-3s.

Tools like the A-3 report are made available to all employees as a key part of their training; they are also shared with suppliers in supplier councils, study groups, and supplier development projects. It's all part of Honda's approach to relationship building, a series of process steps and methods that are executed deliberately, with little left to chance. And the A-3 clearly pays off.

From its first days in Ohio, Honda's purchasing department took a pivotal role in the company, because more than 80 percent of the cost of the vehicles is purchased outside. A purchasing executive sat on the board of directors, and Honda presidents have traditionally had strong purchasing backgrounds. Chairman Yoshino, for instance, who takes a very hands-on approach, had years working in procurement. Unlike most North American chief executives, with the exception of GM's Wagoner and Chrysler's former president Thomas Stallkamp, Yoshino knows when purchasing neglects any key details of the job. For Honda's chief executives, purchasing is definitely on the career path.

Very quickly, Honda's top management tasked the Marysville team with staffing up. But it was not easy to find the right type of purchasing professional, someone who could understand The Honda Way, and someone who would work well building trust relationships, as well as understand the technical requirements. New hires often came not from surrounding mature industries; instead, HAM preferred to bring in new young graduates, train them under Honda veterans, and build expertise and specific technical skills as time went by.

In fact, most purchasing hires came fresh out of regional universities and colleges, like Bowling Green State, Michigan State, and Arizona State, institutions that are known for offering good purchasing programs. Ten or fifteen Japanese managers stayed as the new associates' mentors, transferring their knowledge of process and materials, as well as The Honda Way, to the new employees. The Japanese believe in teaching by doing and showing; in fact, with founder Soichiro Honda, academic credentials counted for little if employees could not prove their technical competence above all else.

This may be an unusual mentoring approach, but Honda executives found it did the job in a very short time. In less than five years, the Honda purchasing organization started gaining national and international recognition from groups such as McKinsey and AT Kearney. By 1995, HAM was recognized as the number one purchasing group in the country, a leader in Best Practices, and a pioneer establishing a new way of putting together a world-class supply management organization.

As the organization grew, two subgroups took shape—a commodity planning and cost management group that were experts in specific parts groups such as plastics, stampings, electronics, and seat assemblies, and a tactical execution group. The first group's job, planning and cost management, was to understand their technology, the market it played in, and pricing details better than the suppliers themselves. As new hires came on board, Japanese mentors would assign a particular commodity to that person, and stay with him or her, quizzing and checking, as the new hire picked up the reins.

The second group inside purchasing covered the tactical side. This group released schedules to meet assembly plant requirements, and interfaced on daily problems, print changes, and so forth. Honda also assigned a Japanese mentor to the tactical side as well, particularly when there were many Japanese suppliers. Terry Maruo, the father of Honda's BP method, taught many young Americans The Honda Way of supplier development. He believed in teaching his trainees on the job, on a supplier project, where he could work on the project team, challenging their assumptions, and continuing to ask them leading questions. Typically, his trainees learned the process well after one or two projects, and they were ready to move out on their own. In the early days of the Marysville operation, one veteran remembers, "You got very smart very fast!"

Purchasing's power position within the corporate hierarchy guaranteed that although requests for additional resources were met with little question, the expectations and visibility placed on purchasing professionals were clearly higher. Purchasing managers were expected to take the lead in new products and other complex projects, as the Acura introduction illustrates.

Purchasing Drives Continuous Improvement

The introduction of the Acura to the Marysville complex exemplifies how design, purchasing, and manufacturing were localized in the North American market. When Marysville took on the Acura project, its first high-end offering, Honda had resident engineers who would regularly, from the very beginning, meet with purchasing planners who were closely involved from concept onward with the new design. Decisions about which technology, which material, and even which suppliers to use were made with engineers at the design stage, and they were tracked for results.

Batteries!

Over time the engineers from Honda, plus engineers from suppliers, got to know each other quite well; they began to communicate with no boundaries. For example, with Honda's supplier of batteries for the Accord and the Civic, purchasing always encountered spirited discussions from the supplier about the Honda shake test, a requirement not found with other U.S. customers. Why was this test more severe than other customers' and did it really matter, they asked?

The usual answer was that in traditional purchasing and engineering at U.S. companies, once a design was released and in production it stayed static; in Honda and its close suppliers, the culture dictated continued improvement. The Japanese have built into their culture the idea that a car or a battery, or an electronic system, is not a "forever" thing. What they see today is not what it will be tomorrow because there will be improvements, and this expectation marks a big difference between transplant and traditional U.S. purchasing engineering work.

A Scalable Approach

High standards from day one can be intimidating to many companies. Too many producers say they cannot afford to build such a big and competent purchasing department like Honda's, and unless they have seen it done before, they find it difficult to imagine bringing suppliers, buyers, and the rest of the operation on board the way this transplant does. In rapid succession, Honda's first North American venture, the Anna motorcycle plant, was followed in a big way by the automotive complex, then other plants around the world. Amazingly, the process was the same at each site, whether it was Mexico, England, or Thailand—each followed the same purchasing game plan.

In Mexico, for example, the plant started with a breakeven build plan of thirty vehicles per day. Marysville started slowly as well and built lines that were capable of producing a vehicle a minute, knowing that in the North American market, dealers would soon demand that rate.

Low-Risk Expansion

Most traditional car companies and their suppliers would gear up to start with one or two automated lines producing one car per minute, but Honda's idea was to move into a new area, start small and steady, line up suppliers, train everyone well, and then expand. It was essential to build the same quality car, the same way in a small plant, as one that would be built in a gigantic modern facility. When the market demanded more than thirty cars per day, the plan—and trained employees and suppliers—made it easy to expand. Honda veterans learned how to double a plant's size very quickly. In 1982, Maryville personnel started a new line that was up and running at full speed by 1984.

Starting small with a smaller investment guarantees that little is lost if the market drops. If the demand explodes, the plant can supplement local production with imports, and rapidly increase production.

Of course, traditional practice questions how any auto plants worldwide could breakeven at only thirty vehicles per day. Would it not be more aggressive to gear up for large volumes from day one, and to set suppliers and a network in place to support big production? But labor rates and pay scales have little to do with the smaller plants' success. It's the employees' project management skills, the way the company plans years ahead, and the fact that good suppliers come on board early. When everyone follows the plan and executes to the A-3, the plants work exactly as expected. In fact, Honda's small plant approach, which includes running different models down the same line, means a producer and its suppliers can do well at much less than the usual 150 to 200 cars per day.

Taking the Longer View, Another Key Payback Component

Japanese producers take a long-term view of everything, and Honda is no different. The company maintains a long-term plan looking at two or three model cycles, and many supplier relationships have exceeded fifty years. If there is an immediate need, the organization will rev up and go into a new market in a hurry—if, for instance, they must beat the competition to market. But, if they are coming in after everyone else, or if they are cash poor, they know that it will be possible to start with thirty vehicles per day, capture 15 or 20 percent of the market, and carry less risk.

Honda Financial Results—The Incredible Payback

The paybacks for Honda's innovative approach are clear, as the company continues to show positive financials and strong market growth. Furthermore, Honda continues to successfully expand its model line up and achieve deeper diversification to compete with mid- and high-end autos, as well as motorcycles, in tough global markets. By the end of April 2003, Japan's number two automaker announced a 17.6 percent net profit increase even as other automakers' North American sales slumped. Sustainable gains like these are impossible to maintain with the traditional confrontational negotiation model that lacks trust, openness, and a willingness to share success and failure. These gains are impossible from a traditional procurement function, like the ones so many North American companies are saddled with. Honda purchasing covers Spend Management, Best Practices, strategic sourcing, and kaizen in a combination that plans and executes good results at home and in the supply base.[3]

It's Not All Technique

To the outside observer, the Honda purchasing operation is a mix of technical expertise, such as the BP kaizen method, The Honda Way umbrella philosophy, and an energetic culture; to that add the fact that Mr. Honda was regarded by his own industry as an outsider, a maverick, and it's clear that Honda is not confined to traditional methods.

For big paybacks, the group relies on its BP process, a rigorous approach to problem solving and execution that dictates what skills must be taught and how teams move through their work. The process works in white-collar areas like engineering and customer administration, as well as out on the production floor. But the Honda approach to organization and human development has a more subjective, philosophical approach as well.

Developing People The Honda Way

Honda employees come to understand the philosophical underpinnings of not just what the company does but how things are done; it's called The Honda Way. All Honda employees learn that respect for the individual, a real approach to people management and development that sounds unbelievably corny and passé, rules every work transaction. Curiously, in the early days, this approach took on an almost cultlike belief as new hires learned in action what respect for people, including outside suppliers, meant as they repeated the tenets of The Honda Way. A common belief in the value of individuals and the importance of doing a job thoroughly and well permeated Honda's entire purchasing operation as rapid growth was facilitated by the mentoring concept.

Out on the floor, where every purchasing associate takes a rotation, The Honda Way dictates how new team members approach their jobs and how important teamwork and cooperative learning really are. Teams of twelve to fifteen men and women work the assembly lines. These are average Americans, Midwesterners, many of whom have come off the farm to work in this plant. Although they all undergo an orientation, their real training comes on the job when they join their teammates. All production jobs are categorized, and fifteen different team members might do fifteen different jobs. The really adept team members learn everyone's job, so that a mature team can build a car with great speed and enthusiasm, and no mistakes.

One Car a Minute

What happens when the new team member arrives? He may be someone who, one team member recalls, "can't put a nut on a bolt! No matter how much dexterity you have, you have got to learn the rhythm, learn the job, and exactly how to do it right every time." That's where the team comes in—all fourteen team members watch every move the new guy makes; when he messes up, they go help. This process goes on for days, with everybody watching the new guy. In about a week, he learns the new job, and in a couple of weeks, he's an expert. Once he gets it right—it takes time to get the body rhythm expected of all team members—pretty soon everyone knows everybody else's job.

In Terry Maruo's purchasing world, he pays a lot of attention to process, to how the job is done, as well as when. Maruo develops a cadence that helps suppliers work to the beat of the line's production rate. Maruo knows that it is essential for lean operations to target the right pace, and without that number in mind, purchasing engineers will not design flows to meet the production line beat.

Delphi has taken a similar approach to building global lean operations that return paybacks worldwide. Several years ago, Delphi embraced the Toyota Production System, another version of lean, with great vigor. Implementing the Toyota System became a mission inside Delphi, a unifier that allowed Delphi to win twenty Shingo Awards. Delphi's award-winning plants look like Japanese plants: They are clean, with everything in its place; people exude the enthusiasm of winners. And Delphi's approach works in factories everywhere around the globe.

Building and Growing Quickly and Quietly

Developing the lean transformation strategy at Delphi started at the top. When asked "Why are you at Delphi?" coauthor Nelson responded, "to take lean to the supply chain." Delphi had excelled at lean in its own factories, but the next step function improvement required involvement of the entire extended value stream.

To accomplish this task, under coauthor Stegner's leadership, the entire global supply management team did a detailed self-assessment of its current situation—comparing themselves to Honda, Toyota, and to the CAPS 10X Best Practice Models. They then went to all key stakeholders—engineering, manufacturing, finance, and other functions, and to the senior management of every division—to discuss face-to-face what expectations existed for supply management that were not being met, and how each area viewed the priority for extending lean to the supply base.

The team then worked through hundreds of pages of notes, and developed a simple eight-step integrated transformation strategy and a supporting three-year business plan to begin implementation.

Resources required to implement the plan were identified, and paybacks analyzed. A simple 3:1 threshold was established as the minimum target and budgets were prepared for expense and returns.

The plan was communicated to senior management and to divisional management, to the top 150 purchasing managers, then to all 1,800 purchasing people globally in a simultaneous Web cast, and Delphi's lean transformation of purchasing was launched.

When Delphi launched its lean initiatives, just a few people in the company recognized that they were heading into something more than simple improvement of production processes. Soon it became clear inside this former GM company that "going lean" meant a lot more than some happy kaizen events and taking out inventory. The entire supply chain of partners and collaborators, as well as managers who had previously handled narrower job responsibilities, would change. And it has.

Nancy Q. Smith, Delphi's global supply management manager of organizational and employee development, emphasizes that Delphi is still in transition. "I think we know some of our gaps and have a plan to get there. Our execution lags behind that plan but we are working to get better every day—everything takes time. We're in a building mode when everybody else is in a cutting mode!" That's an amazing statement for an operation that has executed its way to twenty Shingos, but it is the reality of making big lean changes in an established organization.

How did this complex operation manage to so quickly spread the word and bring thousands of professionals into the lean transition? Marilyn Rowe, global supply management, change management manager, believes that a solid communications plan was key. "We set out to create an understanding of the lean vision and strategy among leadership, and to create consistent feedback and communication in the organization. We are in the early stages. In fact, one view is that Delphi is 'one hundred years old and five years young.'" They understand that the newness of the Delphi spin-off from GM creates youthful opportunities and energy, but there are old habits to unlearn, and that's where success stories, like twenty Shingos, come in. "There is big part of us that feels one hundred. We want people to see progress and have allegiance to that progress."

So where to start on this huge organizational change? Rowe advises that intrepid change-agents begin at a high level, among the top leadership. As Delphi did with its eighteen supply management directors. Rowe advises, "Get them aligned. Our plan for effective change management over two years ago had the directors get involved by doing a survey. They collected data on our key strategies. Next, we put the directors to work to develop Delphi's eight key initiatives and integrate them in the business plan."

Rowe emphasizes the importance of getting people actively involved in their own transformation. Working with Honda veteran and consultant Susan Insley, the group focused particularly on cost management, supplier development, and strategic sourcing. "Susan helped them to open up their perspective and she exposed them to the top strategists, deep thinkers, and that helped them begin to see where this will take Delphi."

The initial education had a great immediate payback, and it continued to grow. Next, Delphi developed an education program for the leaders, and when their top managers visited buyers in factories around the world the message spread quickly that "something is different." Rowe believes this helped supply management directors build their own knowledge base. "It always comes down to the fact that what needs to be done is pretty basic. We have two leaders, Nelson and Stegner, who understand the need for these things, along with top leadership and that's the real difference. They recognize communications as an important function, and they use it well."

Experienced Delphi change agents warn not to rely on trickle-down networking as a realistic and effective communications method. Delphi needed to get 150 global supply management (GSM) managers equally involved, followed by their 1,800 GSM staffers, and knew it would take more formal approaches like quarterly meetings and updates on what global supply management was doing. Warns Rowe, "Cascading doesn't work well. We are trying a very systematic approach to change management. It includes also having meetings between Delphi senior executives and line buyers and managers regularly to surface issues—Delphi Dialogues diagonal slice meetings—talking about what's working, what's not working, and tying it all back to business plan."

Forming the right message, picking the right medium, processing it through each group within the company, then repeating it several times is hard work. It's like being an air traffic controller, eyes glued to the screen, watching for movement and constantly updating your current position, letting the folks who are in your care know you are out there, awake, and watching! People in transition need reassurance as well as a detailed plan, and a positive message surely helps.

And in fact, knowing where your group is at all times is very important, advises Smith, "We need to understand where we are with our people. Right now there is the temptation for people to think we are finished, but we aren't, although things are moving very fast. You see, most of the people have grown up in a bureaucratic system, one that focused on what *can't* be done." Delphi, like so many innovators, is undergoing many changes simultaneously, and one of them means letting people realize the possibilities, the impact that their own work can have on supply chain success.

Delphi is working to create high-level exposure to sensei for the directors who need to link their individual business plan with the overall business plan, for instance. "Making the connection between the individual's business plan and the company's overall business plan shows how to adjust hiring and plan so that we can look at people as a strategic resource. We're actually doing strategic planning for our key jobs and key people. We look at people as a resource, and we understand what ISM's Dr. Robert Kemp taught us—if we don't do things everyday, we get the 'done syndrome.'" Smith doesn't want the celebration of marvelous successes to lead folks to think "mission accomplished" because Delphi, like many supply management pioneers, has even more work to do.

Skills Inventory

Top management accepts that there are huge changes in skills required to support the new business plan. Smith agrees, "We have to think every day that we are responsible to further our knowledge. What we are trying to put together is a multifaceted approach." Global supply management leaders have completed an analysis and a list of skills that the company needs to execute the business plan; it's an ongoing process of evaluating to what extent a skill is needed and how much preparation each contributor has in that area. The next step is to list the gaps, and then prioritize. "Then", says Smith, "we will have identified curriculum focused on closing those gaps with classroom, on the job training, and life experiences."

One critique of the Honda approach to career pathing is that although people got better and better, there was no place for them to be promoted to, and salaries were somewhat flat. Delphi wants to avoid that problem, however, by adjusting levels to encourage and recognize progress. "We want to honor skills development," she confirms. "There have been some folks at Delphi, in the nonexecutive track even—who would have traditionally stopped at eight levels, boxed in by the 'you are either an executive or you are not' syndrome. But some companies have created the opportunity for engineers to be recognized for deep, rich skills—technically competent good professionals who would, in a large company, be in danger of not being recognized for their particular kind of talent."

Creating the supply management curriculum to fill in gaps and move far ahead is a big challenge, with few comprehensive models in sight and available, among them Sony, Deere, and some nonprofit groups like Supply Management Professional Development (SMPD) Network and ISM's CAPS. The folks at Delphi encourage lots of sharing of global processes, as well as benchmarking the best.

"This is challenging," says Smith, "because we are doing things far beyond traditional practice. We need to close the gaps between what we know and what we must know, but it takes time." A special survey given to the directors helped pinpoint targets for improvement; directors were assigned the task of talking to other functional heads, like the head of finance, asking for instance, "What do you think purchasing does well, and what do they not do well?"

Many improvement efforts move forward with parallel tasks as the organization continues to progress. Delphi has hired twenty-six interns, the first step toward establishing two-way relationships with leading universities in targeted fields. The company makes it a rule to assign those students projects that have high visibility and a high return. There are two reasons for this very smart, but unusual approach. First, "There is huge talent out there in the academic world, but also, reaching into colleges and universities," says Smith, ever the change-agent, "opens up the eyes of guys that have been here thirty years." The interns are well managed with defined project focus in key areas of supply management work—no "make-work jobs" here; each intern has an assigned mentor who has clear visibility to their output. Each intern does a final presentation of data and work methods, and that helps everyone see what is actually possible.

"Collaboration with universities is a two-way street," says Smith. "It also allows us to participate in curriculum development with the universities." Delphi considers this another example of good partnership. Working with a short list from previous successful intern experiences, the institutions include Michigan State, Western Michigan, strong in engineering and procurement, Ohio State, Bowling Green State, North Carolina State, Brigham Young, Arizona State, Ivey School, the University of Western Ontario, and others.

The interns are an incredible group of young supply management professionals. In the group of twenty-six, nine are white males, but the rest, says Rowe, are not. The majority of students speak more than one language. One 2005 graduate specializes in moving business to India, a timely and very valuable area of expertise. Delphi works hard to match talent with specific kinds of work; trying to get the students into projects that they love has great payback, and it's an exciting dynamic that builds the two-way relationship with universities.

Change management continues in the lean manufacturing areas so critical to supplier development, as Delphi's lean manufacturing experts help beef up and build awareness. Trips to Toyota, another "Wow!" experience, help executives visualize the impact that new lean methods will have in their own plants. It's all part of pulling together everyone from all the different divisions, to form Team Delphi's high horsepower change vehicle. Being one company means that everyone must have the same information about systems, about what customers think and want, and what makes excellence.

Delphi's new supply management development change objective is for the organization to become a problem-solving culture, rather than a risk-averse, well-padded operation. "We're trying to be agile and execute really well," says Smith, "so that we can be successful, still recognizing there are those that are already quite good at what we want to do. If everybody understands the plan really well and has the skills, you don't have to ask for permission!"

And remember, communications is key. Both managers advise building on strengths to start to move; then, share and teach your progress, and reach every employee. Set high expectations, they urge, and let every buyer understand what the others are doing, because that shows what is possible, what "regular guys" can do!

A Warning About Decentralized Organizational Structures

Honda is centralized in each major region and decentralized globally. There are many reasons, political and historic, why companies use decentralized procurement, but the numbers call for a review of this approach. At John Deere, for instance, where purchasing was able to leverage supplier development and commodity intelligence to cut millions off the spend, a partially decentralized organization structure made it difficult to realize all potential paybacks.

Although purchasing was centralized for planning purposes, out at the division and plant level there remained purchasing directors who reported dotted line to headquarters and solid line to their plants. This structure required new approaches to innovation in Spend Management and other purchasing initiatives.

Conclusion

It takes well-trained people, the right organizational structures, Best Practices, and a few software technology assists to build a high payback supply management group. In this chapter, we recommended that organizations contemplating change first benchmark the best and gather good examples and data from companies like Honda and Delphi and from sources like the 10X CAPS Project. Next, compare these companies' supply management people and operations to theirs and find the gaps. Then, be sure the people are prepared to take on whatever purchasing challenge awaits them, whether it is developing a world-class supply base, as Honda has done so well, or creating a seamless new product introduction cycle. Give the supply management professionals the right tools—good cost management models and the right computer assists—as they start to build their Incredible Payback capabilities, and empower them with high visibility and access to the right tools. We've offered a short list of possibilities in the technology area that can take an organization to high paybacks sooner, and we continue to recommend that supply management teams supplement Best Practice operations with good technology tools.

Finally, in the area of the twenty Best Practices, we have highlighted supplier development as one of the leading high payback practices, investments that invariably has strong paybacks. Honda has provided us with several perspectives on Best Practices, including the A-3 project report, The Honda Way, and cost management, and we looked at how Honda prepares people to work in their high-visibility operation. Building The Incredible Payback operation is an exercise in possibilities, and Best Practice models, including our ten best companies' winners, understand how to combine these four elements—people, organizational structure, and technology assists, plus the discipline of Spend Management—to achieve, three, four, five, and even 10X yields.

Notes

1. CAPS Research, Project 10X Web site, 2001.
2. 2P/3P stands for product and production process preparation, a Japanese technique that uses simulation to see how product and processes work before launch. For more information on 2P/3P, see Anand Sharma and Patricia E. Moody, *The Perfect Engine* (The Free Press: New York, 2003).
3. *Industry Week* Headlines, May 14, 2003, www.industryweek.com.

Chapter 6

Metrics for The Incredible Payback

Y<small>OU'VE BEEN INVITED INTO THE AIR TRAFFIC CONTROL TOWER FOR</small> L<small>OGAN</small> Airport, one of the "movingest" airports in North America—an international center hosting over two dozen air carriers serving commercial and personal travel. Logan started out as a single tin terminal with an observation tower on the roof and one runway on the edge of the salt marsh surrounding Boston Harbor. As the airport grew, the marshes were filled in to accommodate more runways, bigger terminals arranged in U-formation, and more access roads. Still, it wasn't enough. In the 1990s, transportation planners realized that the airport occupied a key trucking transit point for vehicles coming from the South Shore to points north. A way to divert traffic from Boston's crooked clogged streets was needed, and so they designed a tunnel, part one of the Big Dig, under the harbor that would divert thousands of autos away from the hub and run them directly through the airport. Now, the airport had grown from a little landing field where aircraft shared space with seagulls and an occasional owl, to a complex system of people, trucks, cabs, hotels, walkways, distribution centers, and one tower to run it all.

The complexity is blinding, and a single event—a Northeaster or an elevated terrorist threat—disrupts the system and blows everyone's schedule, with planes on the ground, planes circling in the air, maintenance people on hold, plenty of discomfort all around.

But this twenty-first-century relic is not unlike the supply chains that so many of our best businesses work through every day. And like the air traffic controllers working the Logan tower, it all runs on a mix of real-time data, verbal communication, visuals, and luck. Sometimes the weather intervenes, and the customers at Logan and in our supply chains become equally impatient, equally driven by their own demanding schedules.

The controllers can't run Logan Airport on last month's arrival schedule or yesterday's planned departures. How many times would the warning alarms sound if controllers could not see the planes they were tracking on radar, but had to simply rely on day-old dispatches of which 747 took off and which Airbus landed? Under the old input-output theory of manufacturing management, a simple approach to managing the kind of complexity found in most machine shops, for instance, the planner watched only two points—input, where materials entered the system, and output, where they left the dock. Everything in between—each movement of material into a process, all the orders waiting in queue, and everything else—was controlled with a simple priority calculation that gave the hottest items the highest attention.

For air traffic controllers, every flight in between input and output translates to thousands of passengers in the air waiting for a runway. They worry about thousands of passengers five miles up, and good control means knowing the real-time position of every aircraft until it is safely on the ground. Losing track of even one aircraft can be a disaster, but for supply managers, such a nightmare happens to be very much like what they struggle with every day—

not knowing what's in the pipeline, what's really going to be consumed, what's sitting as excess, and where to put it. And what are the price positions? It's not all about inventories, it's about price and risk as well.

Real-Time Control Systems for Real-World Supply Chains

Clearly, Logan Airport Tower runs on a more evolved mix of real-time data bounded by inescapable exception reports—supervisors, buzzers, and alarms—that watch for problems and respond appropriately. And the challenge for the next generation of supply management controllers, who are responsible for moving and processing materials in a web of hundreds of far-flung input and output points, is finding a good mix of simple metrics that tell how the operation is doing, and where a "plane" is headed for trouble. In our Incredible Payback operation, we want to meet profitability goals, as well as run the business well, so the metrics must reflect this key objective.

What are the few but very important metrics that will work best with your supply chain? There are dozens of ratios and tracking numbers that look at all levels of purchasing, manufacturing, and distribution activities, from cutting contracts to scheduling expedited shipping to the income statement, the highest-level monitor of a supply chain's success. Internally and externally, we can measure performance on several key criteria; supplier performance to standard quality, delivery and cost items is well established in most supply chains. We can compare overall financial performance to stated corporate goals, and we can even measure how well personnel policies are working to grow people. In our review of metrics from seven current sources, we were surprised to find *one hundred ninety-one metrics* for supply management, by far more signals than most companies can monitor or respond to, and certainly well in excess of the amount of information a good traffic controller could safely work with.

Manufacturing pioneer Richard Schonberger, the author of best-sellers *Japanese Manufacturing Techniques: Nine Hidden Lessons in Simplicity* and *Let's Fix It! Overcoming the Crisis in Manufacturing,* has been tracking one of our most basic metrics, inventory turns, for more than fifteen years, and he does not like the trends the numbers reflect. Toyota sales continue to rise globally for the twelfth year in a row, despite a case of inventory bloat. Although companies have turned their resources to focus on internal waste with kaizen teams and other lean initiatives, there are even more opportunities outside the factory in the supply chain.

Schonberger knows that a key indicator of corporate health is inventory turns—that is, how well materials move through a complex system. For most North American manufacturers, that was often the only indicator they pursued on their drive to become leaner. But in a complex supply chain, focus on inventory reduction does not necessarily improve service or reduce overall costs. When inventories drop, there should be a boost to cost savings, but big paybacks lie in other, untouched areas as well.

Metrics for The Incredible Payback

Supplier Development[1]

Percent of targets met for supplier lead-time reduction

Percent of targets met for supplier cost reduction

Percent of targets met for supplier quality improvement

Percent of targets met for supplier service improvement

Percent of targets met for supplier technology development

Percent of targets met for supplier usage of total cost of ownership (TCO)

Average spend per active supplier

Percent of supply-base-reduction targets achieved

Percent of active suppliers accounting for X percent of the spend

Number of active suppliers accounting for X percent of purchases

Percent of contracts negotiated under single source

Percent of suppliers with 100 percent lot acceptance for one year

Percent of supplies delivered on schedule

Suggestions submitted—number, dollars, and percent of total spend

Financial Measures

Total inventory in days or weeks

Percent of time inventory days of supply target met

Direct material purchases as percentage of COGS

Percent of total contracts spend versus all direct materials spend

Actual purchased materials cost per budgeted cost

Labor hours per $10,000 purchases

Cost savings using P-card purchasing

Cost of rush/expedited orders

Percent of targets met for reduction of expedited orders

Percent of discount orders by consolidating orders

Percent projected cost reductions missed

Cost-to-spend ratio

Stocking costs

Procurement Professional Performance

Active suppliers managed per purchasing professional

Percent of global sourcing targets met

Percent of suppliers rated for quality, delivery, service, and lead time

Percent of purchasing professionals using Web procurement for X percent of purchases

Percent/number of items for which purchasing discovered a second source

Percent of targets met for joint decisions between procurement and engineering

Customer satisfaction rating

Customer quality rating

Customer responsiveness rating

Warranty issues or resolutions

Training hours per person

Inventory turns by category

Number of cost models in place and agreed to

Various Measures of Engineering Collaboration

System compatibility, progress on collaborative design programs, measures of part standardization, and part reuse

Technology insertion measures, including rate of new technology review and proposed, usefulness of ideas

Operational Measures

Average time to fill emergency orders

Average time to replace rejected lots with good parts

Errors per purchase order

Expeditors per direct employees

Number of items billed but not received

Number of items on the hot/short/allocation list

Number of orders received with no purchase order

Parts costs per total costs

Percent decrease in parts cost

Purchase order cycle time

Number of times per year line is stopped due to lack of
supplier parts

Routing and trace errors per shipment

Percent of defect-free supplier model parts

Percent of lots received on line late

Percent of parts with two or more suppliers

Percent of purchase orders returned due to errors or
incomplete description

Time required to process the equipment purchase orders

Time to answer customer complaints

Supplier parts scrapped due to engineering changes

Percent of purchases using P-cards

Percent of total spend using P-cards

Percent of non-compliant P-card purchases

Percent of orders qualified for P-card but P-card not used

Contract monitoring/compliance

Contract volume purchased/volume commitment

Contract dollar purchased/dollar commitment

Percent purchases compliant with contract price

Quality reject rate versus contract specification

Percent on-time deliveries versus contract spec

Percent days supplier inventory level within contract spec

Returns volume/allowed returns

Change orders implemented and compliant with contract spec

Warranty commitments honored

Unscheduled downtime

Material availability service measures

Maintenance cost reductions

Downtime due to product performance

Response time

Quality (ppm) and first-time quality

Number of quality alerts

Delivery performance

Productivity improvement (typically pieces per hour before and after)

Takt time

Health and safety improvements

Consistent worldwide service, as indication of flexibility and ability to move work

Stable lead times

Manufacturing cycle time reduction

Order processing time reduction

Percent sourced to preferred suppliers

Alignment—degree to which customer and supplier organizations are in agreement on basic philosophies

Air traffic control systems are designed to manage a few mission-critical events; the controller assumes that the inventory he manages is designed and well-maintained to get the job done. Other goals, such as time-to-service aircraft on turnaround and time required to find a parking place, may affect aircraft on-time departures, and so they also become part of the real-time control system, although air traffic dispatchers cannot direct them. In fact, all the activities of a complex supply chain in some way have an impact on achieving The Incredible Payback. The question, however, is which metrics should a supply chain in its current development stage use? Traditional organization goals and metrics will track different indicators from those managed by expert operations that have conquered all the basics.

Procurement departments fall into three or four different maturity phases: Phase 1—Getting Started, Phase 2—Most Procurement Functions, Phase 3—Excellent Procurement, and Phase 4—Almost Perfect Procurement. During each one of these stages, the corporation looks to procurement to help improve bottom-line performance. Throughout the changes most companies have seen in procurement, more responsibility has shifted to procurement. The metrics best used in each of the four phases need to be well selected and maintained, but they also must be good preparation for moving to the next performance level.

Phase 1: Getting Started, Traditional Operations

Phase 1 operations tend to be transaction driven, buried in paperwork, with changing priorities, shortages, and delivery and quality problems making purchasing operations more tactical than strategic. A tough business climate will often drive the Phase 1 operation to get expedites under control and to conquer pricing, even though the operation usually does not know what the total spend is, or how the money is being spent with specific suppliers.

Metrics for the Phase 1 operation looking to move forward would include the following:

- ❑ Unscheduled downtime
- ❑ Material availability
- ❑ On-time delivery
- ❑ Inventory turns

❑ Shortages
❑ Quality:
  ❑ ppm, first-time quality, PPAP 100 percent on-time and complete, major disruptions, customer disruptions
❑ Purchased price variance?

Phase 2: Most Procurement Functions, Beginners

Phase 2 operations show considerable improvement over Phase 1 beginners, as most major commodity groups are being leveraged. Most buying transactions have been automated, not necessarily over the Internet. Buyers attend professional training directly related to their work. Internal price monitoring has brought prices under control, and what is negotiated with the supplier is what is actually paid. Operations may still be primarily tactical, but planning is beginning to have stronger influence over the way the supply chain operates, at least in key commodity areas.

Some suppliers are certified and some maintain excellent communications and partnering, trust relationships with the customer. Suggestion systems and other joint improvement efforts are under discussion and may be in initial stages with a few notable success stories.

The organization will still measure quality and on-time deliveries, as well as pricing, but as the group adds more strategic commodity or market intelligence to the buyer/planner job, other bigger issues become equally important.

Metrics for the Phase 2 operation include the following:

❑ Suggestions submitted for continuous improvement, number selected and acted upon, and dollar value of suggestions
❑ Quality:
  ❑ ppm, first-time quality, PPAP 100 percent on-time and complete, number of major quality disruptions
❑ Number of suppliers in total, and by commodity globally

❑ Percentage of qualified suppliers
❑ Percentage of items or spend dedicated to single/dual source
❑ Inventory reduction compared with goals, measured in turns, weeks, or days on hand, and dollars by specific category (for example, obsolescence dollars), or inventory turns compared with industry average/industry best
❑ Number of hours training per year per buyer/planner

Phase 3: Excellent Procurement, Experts

The Phase 3 supply management group does more than purchase and control inbound materials. This group is prepared to work with the supply base to share improvement methods with suppliers. The supply base in a Phase 3 operation has been trimmed to no more than five suppliers per commodity, and includes a manageable group of high-performing suppliers with whom the customer hopes to maintain long-term agreements. Although problems in quality and delivery can happen, they are not everyday occurrences and both partners are prepared to deal with most crises.

Supplier selections are made not only on price but also on quality, delivery, technical contribution, and leadership. Each commodity has a written strategic plan that sets out price, supplier, and technology planning.

The supply managers reach beyond traditional purchasing limits and work closely with engineers and designers, and also suppliers, on new product introductions. Purchasing's contribution to these teams is commodity and cost expertise, as well as thorough understanding of possible supply base partners.

Metrics for the Phase 3 operation include the following:

❑ The usual quality, delivery performance statistics
❑ Savings generated by supplier development, or new product purchasing involvement

❏ Comparison of prices obtained by commodity teams to industry price index and global price trends
❏ Annual spend savings compared with corporate reduction goal
❏ Cost models and cost targets for most major commodity areas

Focus on future proactive measures, such as:

❏ *New model launch*—Quality/part maturation
❏ *New model launch*—Project plan/gate reviews met
❏ *New model launch*—Cost targets achieved

Phase 4: Almost Perfect Procurement, Advanced

The Phase 4 operation is a rare example of highly paid and well-trained supply management professionals who understand manufacturing as well as purchasing, the right computer systems, the best-of-the-best suppliers, and innovative compensation schemes that reward best performance.

IBM and Honda are companies with Phase 4 operations. The supply chain management function is integrated and covers all aspects of buying, processing, and shipping product. Manufacturing and distribution may report to the head of the supply chain.

The goals and practices of the Phase 4 supply management group are well aligned with corporate objectives. If the corporation decides to seize new market technology share, supply management can quickly ramp up to acquire suppliers who are able to meet the exploding demand. If the market is more mature, and corporate plans include better margins on mature products, purchasing will be expert at worldwide price negotiation.

Phase 4 suppliers have near-perfect processing, and they have developed strong abilities to flex with customer demands. On the customer side of the supply chain, the advanced operation is consistently ranked by its supplier surveys as their number one customer.

Computer systems in the advanced operation include a well-integrated mix of strategic and tactical technology tools that integrate engineering and manufacturing with purchasing and the supply base. Implementation of new technology tools happens quickly—in less than one year—and at lower price points. All functions are working with the same integrated B.O.M. structure, although they may have visibility to limited segments of the bill. Cost Management is well established on an integrated database that drives purchasing strategies and paybacks.

Exchange Rate Tracking/Risk Management

Phase 4 buyers are aware of currency fluctuations in the major markets, and they may use that information to find advantageous prices. One Midwestern purchasing chief meets monthly with the treasurer and sales vice president to study their major currency markets, and determines where the risks to current best prices are. Last year, for example, this company would have lost money, but because of its global buying and selling operations, the company cleared an additional 1 percent by proactive hedging of currency exposure. It's not a random roll of the dice, but a deliberate selection of certain areas to buy from. In some years, the exchange rate is so good that planners can eliminate most of their currency risk. In fact, the purchasing chief has been able to wring an additional 1 percent out of spend reductions simply by tracking currency swings.

Generally, companies moving from traditional practices start to gather useful metrics by tracking quality and delivery performance, then adding other critical measures—cost and Spend Management, best customer ranking, and new product measures—as they develop expertise. It's amazing how much difficulty most supply chains have gathering the kind of good basic performance and spend data they need to make informed decisions. Starting with basic purchasing performance, including supplier tracking, the metrics are simple. Moving to continuous improvement project monitoring for kaizen teams, purchasers add a few more key indicators to the basics. The biggest payoff metrics are those that track the whole area of Cost Management by offering savvy purchasers a new world of competitive costs.

For the Allied Corporation Income Statement example, we showed how a spend reduction goal of 10 percent could be used to create new shareholder returns, new plants and products, or simply a reduction in the spend. Allied's supply management must perform at the expert or advanced level to achieve this level of savings consistently year after year. Also, the metrics to meet the spend reduction must track spending at the commodity and part number levels compared with industry indices, as well as engineering and distribution.

Allied's current income statement showed 88 percent of its revenues spent on purchased materials and services, as well as manufacturing; the rest went to engineering, R&D, and SG&A, leaving nothing for profits. If the head of supply management controls Allied manufacturing (outsourced and internal) and engineering, as well as purchasing and distribution, the 10 percent target will be easier to achieve and sustain. Either way, it is important to verify, track, and control (VTC) the savings with the right metrics so that they don't disappear from one budget only to pop up in another expense area. Although the income statement may be generated quarterly, more frequent tracking to specific savings goals will sharpen commodity buying and supplier activities.

 Allied Income Statement

Revenue from sales	$2.5 billion
Cost of goods sold:	

Cost of purchased goods and
services (55 percent of sales)   1.375 billion

Manufacturing in-house
(33 percent of COGS)   .825

Engineering and R&D (6 percent)   .15

SG & A (Selling, General and
Administrative) (6 percent)   .15

Profit   0

Five year plan for 10 percent savings = $.25 billion, or 50 million/year.

Key to any supply management group achieving and tracking payback is first of all Cost Management. Japanese producers are expert at gathering and sustaining the kind of detailed cost information that allows planners to make competitive decisions about suppliers and new parts. Strong Cost Management is what allowed both Honda and Toyota to take costs in their four-door sedans down by nearly 25 percent. A few North American organizations are learning the Japanese approach to cost modeling and cost targeting; Delphi, the GM spin-off, is one of them.

Cost Management to Achieve Incredible Payback

Tom Stuart, cost manager and lead engineer for powdered metal commodity planning and control, reports to Delphi's new cost expert, Toyota veteran Hiromichi Kamimura, the director of Cost Management. Although Delphi has always had some good Cost Management practices, Kamimura brought a new level of expert planning to this crucial element of The Incredible Payback.

Stuart's role, which is to support new products in the design stage, helps guarantee that the supplier has the right processes and the right "should cost." He works hand in hand with the commodity team manager to ensure that his cost goals align with the purchasing objectives. As the corporate expert in sintered metals, Stuart's influence cuts across divisions and specific products. He gathers prints, selects the right materials, and recommends suppliers to the commodity manager. On a new product, says Stuart, "We can come to agreement on the materials and the prototype, so that when we go to the supplier for their quote, we hand them the process, and we already know that the target cost and the price are the same. When we talk about 'should cost,' that cost should reflect Best Practices in my industry around the world." Once the team picks a supplier, they work with them, let them know what the worldwide cost is on the part, and "if I need a lean team or supplier development to help, we'll do it."

The entire method of handling powdered metal revolves around material and processing intelligence that Stuart hopes will not be lost as people retire, because it's critical to building a competitive advantage. When Stuart goes out for quotes, he asks for a price breakdown sheet with the quote that identifies the material and processes the supplier proposes to use. "That also gives me a cost breakdown of what they are charging us to do. We gather all this data and roll it into the database, which allows the team to look at the industry for a particular area, for instance, what the average press operator is making. It's so important to have the data, because not knowing costs for worldwide markets can destroy profitability."

The model is built on an Excel spreadsheet, but Stuart is looking to move it to more powerful software because cost experts need the ability to model and study more complex processes, like stamping. Planning is dependent on Stuart's function to give them information that will help pick the right supplier, because, Stuart warns, "it doesn't bother me to go with a supplier that costs more. We may find out that just by putting parts in India, we pay a little higher cost, but we get good quality, people are well trained, and that's better than going to a low-price supplier but not knowing what you're paying for." He predicts that the supply base may grow as planners study Poland, Korea, China, and other low-cost countries. Delphi likes to look at suppliers that have operations in other countries because that lessens the customer's risk and improves flexibility.

Stuart warns that industry and technical knowledge is just as important as financial expertise, because suppliers respect a delicate balance of process and materials that the cost models help to maintain.

Stuart's influence on costs through supplier selection, development, and even new product design is considerable. His function is the bridge connecting corporate income statement goals with savings targets. This is how he describes the process, "Basically, I am building a cost model with my experience. We look globally to find the best price for the processes we run in different countries because we want the best price for the product." His work includes reviewing current suppliers on the bid list as well, to evaluate their processes, their materials, the quality, and location. For instance, when engineering releases a new part, Stuart reviews and studies it from all angles.

Once Stuart selects a supplier, the contract is written to include cost waste reduction and sharing of savings throughout the life of the contract. If the current supplier quote is higher than Stuart's global cost model, or "should cost," that's when supplier development or lean teams take over to get costs in line with targets.

Things are changing in the powdered metals area as new materials take entire processing steps out of the technology.

One lesson in this new approach to Cost Management is the importance of establishing good data sources and preserving the intelligence from one model and one technology to the next. Good cost modelers prefer to build on previous expertise, rather than start out fresh with each new idea.

Data Sources

Basic quality, delivery, comparative cost, and cost target data are foundation requirements for performance and cost improvement tracking. The data can initially be constructed from receipts and contract or purchase order information on file. For daily tracking, ERP or purchasing receiving and accounts payable systems should capture the actuals. We recommend a minimum of three years' history. Best Practice enterprises and their suppliers, like Harley-Davidson, Honda, and Deere, can access from a combination of sources of good performance data.

Some advanced operations are using software to gather and package good metrics. For example, Intellimet and Valuedge supplier assessment solutions are used to identify and report supplier data that eliminates the need for multiple audits. The software can establish a baseline of supplier performance against which future benchmarks are compared. Some software providers offer Web-enabled solutions that help to standardize and accelerate the rate of adoption throughout the enterprise.

Cost data that rolls up for comparison to income statement goals helps supply chain managers to stay on target. But supply chain managers still need to decide which portions of the purchasing spend will deliver the greatest payback and get closest to the corporate savings objective. Some companies, particularly those in Phase 1 and Phase 2 stages, will use supplier development to take waste out of manufacturing processes and inventory. Operations that are more advanced, such as Phase 3 and Phase 4 organizations, will be able to use strategic global sourcing and Spend Management to make better sourcing decisions. Advanced operations will be working with detailed accurate cost models and new product engineering to take costs out before they happen.

Next, we will look at how Delphi's business strategy transformed the supply chain.

Planning and Delivering The Incredible Payback: How Delphi's Business Strategy Transformed the Supply Chain

Delphi's Strategic Intent: To achieve competitive advantage through extended value stream excellence.

When Delphi decided to address supply chain opportunities with a full-blown business strategy session, planners knew that with a well-conceived and detailed execution plan, they would strike gold. And they did.

Delphi's rigorous strategic planning process takes the corporate supply chain vision—"To be recognized by our customers as their best supplier!"—and translates that broad statement into successively more-detailed plans and metrics, which is the only way to guarantee the team will achieve its objective. The strategy is extended into a three-year plan supported by more-detailed one-year business plans that link to detailed action plans for corporate, the division, specific commodity groups, and regions. All bases are covered (see Figure 6–1).

Strategic plans are supported by the following eight integrated elements, or tactical operating areas, that require intensive and detailed execution and resources:

1. Supplier development
2. Cost management
3. Strategic sourcing
4. Quality improvement
5. Systems infrastructure
6. People development
7. Supplier relationships
8. Management of change

Each one of the eight areas is covered by a three-year strategy. For instance, in Supplier Development, a high-payoff area, year

The Business Plan templates provide a link between strategic intent and the individual performance

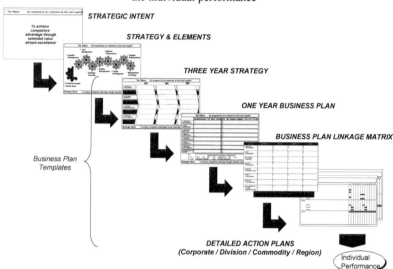

STRATEGIC INTENT

STRATEGY & ELEMENTS

THREE YEAR STRATEGY

ONE YEAR BUSINESS PLAN

BUSINESS PLAN LINKAGE MATRIX

Business Plan Templates

DETAILED ACTION PLANS
(Corporate / Division / Commodity / Region)

Individual Performance

Figure 6–1. Business plan.

one calls for lean launches and early successes. Year two expands Supplier Development to more suppliers with significant cost reductions, and year three shows continued expansion, plus integration of Strategic Sourcing with the new area of Cost Management, the best combination to achieve the biggest cost savings.

Cost Management, a new and very high potential area for Delphi, is scheduled to grow in three years from a bare bones operation to one that covers all commodities and all stages of product development.

The strategic sourcing element will define and identify key suppliers and later integrate with other disciplines to achieve supply objectives. The same focused approach is taken with Quality Improvement, Systems Infrastructure, People Development, Supplier Relationships, and Change Management. Each one of these transformation areas is accompanied by metrics that tie results di-

Business Plan

The Vision: *Be recognized by our customers as their best supplier!*		
	(A) MANAGING THE BASE BUSINESS	**(B) TRANSFORMING FOR THE FUTURE**
1. SUPPLIER DEVELOPMENT		
2. COST MANAGEMENT		
3. STRATEGIC SOURCING		
4. QUALITY IMPROVEMENT		
5. SYSTEMS INFRASTRUCTURE		
6. PEOPLE DEVELOPMENT		
7. SUPPLIER RELATIONSHIPS		
8. MANAGEMENT OF CHANGE		
	BUSINESS RESULTS	
Strategic Intent: *To achieve competitive advantage through extended value stream excellence*		

Figure 6–2. Business plan template.

rectly to project plans, and each one of these metrics rolls up to overall financial objectives (see Figures 6–2 and 6–3).

On Supplier Development, for example, the task is to staff up at the corporate level, including hiring supplier development engineers. At the division level, planners will identify suppliers for development projects, and then follow up by monitoring and tracking savings, a key contributor to the VTC process. It is at the commodity level that savings are delivered and tracked. Finally, at the regional level, supplier support and prioritization helps to ensure that planners are working on the right supplier issues.

The details of Supplier Development's task at the corporate level of launching lean is a minimum of twenty-five suppliers appearing in Figure 6–3. In each of the eight elements' detailed action plan, like Supplier Development's template shown in Figure 6–4 on facing pages 232 and 233, key metrics track progress against objectives. For example, Figure 6–4 tracks lead-time re-

Business Plan Linkage Matrix – Design

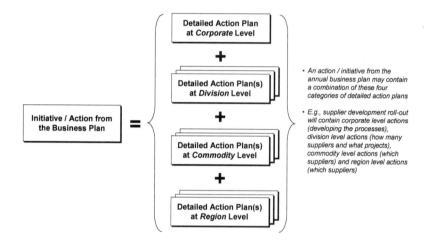

Business Plan Linkage Matrix – Actions by element

ELEMENT	CORPORATE	DIVISION	COMMODITY	REGION
• SUPPLIER DEVELOPMENT				
• COST MANAGEMENT				
• STRATEGIC SOURCING				
• QUALITY IMPROVEMENT				
• SYSTEMS INFRASTRUCTURE				
• PEOPLE DEVELOPMENT				
• SUPPLIER RELATIONSHIPS				
• MANAGEMENT OF CHANGE COMMUNICATION				

Figure 6–3. Business plan linkage matrix—design.

duction against a corporate target of 30 percent. Supplier Development should achieve from three-to-one savings, up to ten to one. Delphi hopes to achieve six-to-one payback because the company is starting with experienced staff.

Finally, for comparison with last year's achievements, Figure 6–5 on page 234 pulls up the previous template—the 2002 Business Plan—showing how well Global Purchasing performed against its total mission. Figure 6–5 shows that on indirect material and direct material performance, all goals were met.

Delphi's rigorous and comprehensive approach to planning for success has parallels in other areas of strategic change. Marketing would use the same approach to plan for growth in new products or new markets; manufacturing handles increased capacity needs by breaking down the overall need into dozens of little actions that must happen to achieve overall success. The same approach was taken for the quality crusades of the 1980s. Supply chain managers have experienced most of these hard marches, and they are experts at applying the same techniques to bringing higher performance to the supply chain. It's a detailed approach that, in the end, makes everything look easier and smoother, but without such rigorous planning, the risks around obtaining big paybacks inevitably increase.

Conclusion

"Let the numbers lead you."

—Dorian Shainin, 1914–2000, Shewhart Award winner

Every day, in every little business that makes things, a terribly long list of possible events that can go wrong do just that—the parts don't show up, or they don't work, they look ugly, or they cost too much. Your system should be designed to lead to answers and recovery plans, and so picking the right metrics is critical not only

Department/Process Name:

Policy Objective / Outcome	Objective, Action Item	Responsible	Target Area / Project

Legend

Control Point	△		Completed	▲
Start Planned	○		Actual	●
Completion Planned	○		Actual	●

Figure 6–4. Action plan corporate-level template.

| Owner: |
| Approver: |
| Date: |

Timeline	>	>	>	>	>	>	>	>	>	>	Review
Jan	Feb	Mar	Apr	May	June	July	Aug	Sept	Oct	Nov	Dec	Initials & Date

Initials

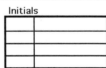

Figure 6–4. Action plan corporate level template (*cont.*).

Business Plan Objectives

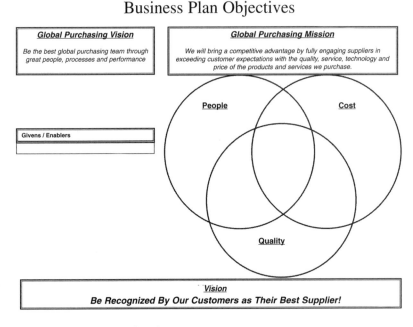

Figure 6–5. Business plan objectives.

because of the behaviors they engender but also the solutions the numbers offer.

There are hundreds of ways to measure supply chain performance, but most expert operations select the right measures for their particular goals—quality, service, or cost reductions—and follow the numbers carefully. The closer enterprise planners can get to building a real-time control system supported by solid reporting, the more responsive the system will be to unpredicted events. Select the areas where your organization will need to ratchet up its performance goals, and look one step beyond to the next metrics that will help move the operation to the next performance level.

Note

1. Thanks to Marsha Begun of Begun Consulting, for sharing her "Key Purchasing Performance Measures"; also to Gene Richter, former CPO of IBM.

Chapter 7

Incredible Payback Conclusions

IT'S A TOUGH TIME FOR MANUFACTURERS EVERYWHERE—NEW, UN-expected challenges pop up every day. No one in supply chain or manufacturing is unaffected by the rapid shifts in markets and supply sources, yet, this particular time is one of great opportunity for the best supply managers who have prepared their organizations well. Every industry faces demand for better performance—lower prices, expanded markets, and more innovation. The automotive sector, for example, is at the tail end of a consolidation binge that started in the 1990s; the electronics and consumer goods sectors are looking for quick recovery, as are retail and construction. Interest rates and consumer buying will do their part to boost sales. But we believe that producers themselves can do a great deal to help themselves.

The network of global producers is so widespread and difficult to take in at a single glance, it's clear to us that we are poised at the edge of enormous supply management potential and power. Every complex supply chain is made up of several hundred suppliers.

The whole galaxy of raw material processing and shipments totals billions of dollars, and from that unexamined opportunity area, smart producers can easily extract 1 or 2 percent savings without any significant new investment.

The challenge, however, for most producers whose supply chains stretch over wide global networks, is to pick a reasonable savings target, and to consistently deliver, and then raise the target level another notch. Most companies have not touched the limits of their payback performance, and we think that even the most traditional operations will be excited and encouraged by the possibilities.

Planning a Time Frame for The Incredible Payback

Once your company has made the big decision to move forward and go for the bigger returns, how long should it take the average purchasing group to prepare and achieve The Incredible Payback? Although we've said that some categories of spend— MRO, for instance—offer quick savings opportunities, other areas will take longer to position for savings, particularly in traditional operations. However, even traditional purchasing operations can consolidate supply sources and find good savings opportunities. All it takes is some planning and some good data, and one or two good leaders.

The opportunities extend beyond simply saving on purchased materials, and we know that many more supply chains will move toward even bigger solutions once they have primed the pump with smaller returns. The planning time frame should be three to five years at least, longer for more strategic changes. We're always struck by the short-sighted responses to big economic downturns and month-to-month or quarter-to-quarter "strategies." Some companies live with the ups and downs of their industry, but for others, every cyclical decline is an entirely new, unplanned-for experience. Operations with longer perspectives understand that they will not only be flipped around by market swings, they may actually, when they have great visibility into their supply chains and strong suppliers, be able to influence their own customers' demand responses.

We've talked about the need for companies to staff up—with people and systems—and to maintain high-level relationships between customers and suppliers, to be prepared to find great payback opportunities. The Best Practice models, companies like IBM, Honda, and Delphi, have perfected most of the methods that take waste out of the supply chain and leverage the power of a large corporate spend. It's simply a matter of seeing what opportunities are out there—to find the appropriate solutions and reel them in.

Realistically, then, a good time frame that encourages more creative results should start with a five-year time horizon and work backward to year one. Plan for one year of scoping out the problem—data digging that describes the opportunities, along with initial savings efforts. Years two and three can be dedicated to perfecting the particular solutions appropriate for the target, and years four and five should continue the savings as the operation ratchets up its performance to the next level. Although any supply management operation can achieve good savings in less than a year, sustained spend reductions along with quality and service improvements are the goal. By year three, functions outside procurement should see and understand the strategy and the numerical results.

Supply Management Payback Opportunities: Savings, Risk Management, and Demand Management

Achieving a minimum 1 percent savings a year is completely possible, even for traditional operations. Moving up to 3 to 5 percent takes focus and persistence, and will require adopting Best Practices, including Spend Management. Traditional operations can achieve savings in this range, but they will find it hard to sustain them year after year without bringing in Best Practices or otherwise changing their organization structure. But achieving annual savings above 5 percent is a level of performance a few excellent companies, such as IBM and Honda, have proven can be done.

Along with Best Practices and targeted savings comes the added challenge of managing risk in the supply chain. Here, supply managers have the ability to mitigate the impact of seasonal swings and economic downturns. They can prevent the wide-reaching financial ripples that have proven disastrous for many operations. Or they can anticipate currency shifts and try to flex the supply chain accordingly.

There is one more new and significant contribution to profitability from supply management—market and demand management. We showed in Chapter 5 how to use software to execute demand management at the supply chain level. Good planning and market intelligence will allow procurement managers to go one step further toward increased financial returns. By allowing managers to study demand flows, supply managers can deliberately ship the right finished product to the right customer or market region, and sales will increase.

Our Approach

Our approach to The Incredible Payback assumes that supply managers are willing to take another look at their suppliers and start building relationships not only on trust and good intentions but also on good data. Continuous improvement—kaizen, The Toyota Production System, and the Honda BP method—will all yield better performance, but they are only beginning results.

Bigger sustained results come from Spend Management. The example of Allied Auto that we used in Chapter 1 illustrates how decreasing the purchasing spend returns cash to corporate coffers, cash that can be used to develop new products, new markets, and even new plants. Starting with the strong savings that can be achieved on the shop floor at just about every supplier's shop, it's easy to see momentum building.

A third approach, one that helps to sustain savings, requires operations to optimize the supply chain. Do not assume that your supply chain network is structured correctly or that it includes all the right suppliers, from raw material down through travel and transportation networks and providers. Even if your planners have rationalized the supplier list down to a manageable three hundred to five hundred suppliers, the distribution pattern and schedules may not be as efficient or cost effective as they could be. Sometimes, as the Deere MRO story illustrates, companies inherit suppliers—they may not be the best, but they're there, and change is difficult. Here we recommended using technology—optimization software or simulations—to try out other scenarios to see what restructuring the supply chain would cost in time and money.

Ten Common Mistakes

Sometimes the best way to begin an improvement project is to identify key problem areas. The exercise of reviewing supply management operations and people, as well as key data, takes some time—a month or two—but it saves premature or wasted starts, or picking the wrong improvement area. It also gives management an opportunity to understand the workings of an area in which most high-level executives spend no time—purchasing and manufacturing processes. The easier it becomes for managers to see the right priorities, the stronger their support (and budgets!) will be.

In Chapter 2, we identified ten common mistakes (see Figure 7–1) that limit payback potential, including organization structures that conflict or overlap, missing and bad data, and bad practices. All these problems create waste and make change that much more difficult. But worst of all, lack of data makes Spend Management a tougher challenge than it should be.

A quick survey of the enterprises' capabilities will reveal whether the customer and its suppliers operate at kindergarten, high school, or Ph.D. levels (see Figure 7–2).

1. Low expectations
2. Decentralized purchasing
3. Production reporting into operations or marketing
4. Lack of good analytical tools
5. Supplier proliferation
6. Short-term, low-level tactical focus
7. Bad press
8. Product variety and complexity
9. No connection or communications between purchasing and new poduct development
10. No supplier development

Figure 7–1. Ten common mistakes.

1. How is procurement organized currently?
   A. Logistics?
   B. Production planning and control?
   C. Incoming material and component quality?
   D. Inventory management?

2. What performance metrics are available currently?
   A. Are they used directly in performance reviews?

3. Who really selects the sources:
   A. Procurement? (Central? Regional? Plant?)
   B. Engineering?
   C. Top management?
   D. If it depends on the commodity, cite some examples.

4. Who negotiates the price and other contract terms?

5. How are make/buy decisions made?
   A. Components?
   B. Finished products?

6. What are the major outside sourced part categories, *based on dollars spent*?

7. What part categories are most critical from a quality, technology, and/or delivery standpoint?

8. Who are the ten most important suppliers? For each, identify:

A. The primary country of manufacturing origin
B. The country of headquarters
C. How often they are visited by procurement people

9. Can your MRP system requires be:
   A. Cross-communicated within the company?
   B. Consolidated into one demand on the supplier?
   C. Nationally?
   D. Globally?

10. What are company policies regarding:
    A. Ethics
    B. Buyer behavior
    C. Supplier behavior, etc.

11. Are there regular, formal processes for communicating with suppliers and getting their input?
    A. Periodic surveys?
    B. Advisory councils?
    C. Ombudsman?

12. Averages of procurement people:
    A. Years of education?
    B. Predominate discipline?
    C. Years with the company?
    D. Years in procurement?

13. What delegation of financial authority do the various levels of procurement have? Does any other function have procurement delegation authority?

SOURCE: R. Gene Richter, former chief procurement officer, IBM Corporation, copyright 2001.

Figure 7–2. Preliminary production procurement questions.

Your operational review will allow you to understand the implications of decentralized/centralized structures, the problem with maverick buying, and the role manufacturing plays in the supply chain, as well as where processing (manufacturing) should report. The good analytical tools that your planners will need for Spend Management and supplier evaluation are key to data gathering, and an audit following Chapter 2 recommendations will uncover data sources and gaps.

A Word About Complexity

Theresa Metty, chief procurement officer of Motorola Cellular, believes complexity is expensive. When she launched her War on Complexity, she knew that Motorola's supply chain operation could yield millions of dollars in savings if purchasing could find ways to collaborate with engineers, manufacturing, and suppliers. The result of her pioneering work made Motorola Cellular the most profitable division in the corporation, and saved billions, as it built supply management's power base.

Complexity is a nasty evil that simply grows and grows until its branches and tendrils reach every part of the supply chain, choking off innovation and standardization. Metty realized that by narrowing down the number of parts that would be used to run generation after generation of new products, Motorola would also strengthen its supply base as suppliers became more adept at producing fewer and cheaper components.

The complexity battle is a tough one that most appropriately belongs to smart supply chain professionals who want to correct complexity waste and contribute to longer-term savings.

Wrap Manufacturing and New Products into the Supply Chain

Theresa Metty's span of responsibility included both manufacturing and the supply chain, and the combination allowed her great advantage over complexity issues. Just as manufacturing belongs in the supply chain organization structure, so must new product development be more carefully linked to supply management. The late Gene Richter, IBM's chief procurement officer, worked especially hard at new product integration at both IBM and Hewlett Packard. He believed that 90 percent of the cost of new products was decided early in the design stage, and he wanted buyers actively involved at that point. Richter's dream was to see software solutions that offer parallel data streams to purchasing, new products, and manufacturing professionals, all drawn from the same data base. Richter maintained high and visible involvement in many new software start-ups and their boards to help move them in that direction and his work influenced the architecture of supply chain systems.

Building a Fair Advantage and Capturing The Incredible Payback

Your operation has reviewed practices, and evaluated what would be reasonable paybacks, including spend reductions. The next step is to build a good foundation on which the group can start to see returns as it moves toward a higher performance level. We have outlined the basics that must be in place—including curiosity and fear—to begin to build a supply management operation that can achieve Incredible Paybacks. What are the absolute essential foundation blocks that must be in place to reach this higher performance level? First, Cost Management, followed by a report card on suppliers, and evaluation of supplier alignment, and a statement of how well the partners work together, or wavelength. Clearly, although not all the foundation work is objective, even developing better soft skills in "fuzzy areas" will be measurable through results, including surveys.

In Chapter 3, we listed the procurement methods that must be added to an operation to move up and achieve higher savings. For beginners, we recommend supplier consolidation and suggestion systems to achieve 1 percent savings. Here we also emphasize the importance of good cost and spend data, a basic requirement that many groups operate without. There is no substitute for good numbers, and supply chain leaders such as Toyota and Honda work hard at building good market and cost intelligence. In this chapter, we also paint the picture of a young high-growth medical products leader, Respironics, starting to restructure its supply chain. The Respironics group illustrates momentum and encouraging savings that were achieved just from working the basics.

Strategic Sourcing's 7 Steps take the foundation elements into daily practice that will earn savings. Starting with the numbers, we recommend a commodity team approach to developing strong expertise. Each commodity and critical part needs a written strategy that covers price, technology, and market trends. Strategic Sourcing requires customers to work with suppliers on cost issues, as well as risk management and recovery plans. Finally, to maintain the gains from year to year, we recommend Step 5: Verify Track, and Control; the only way to track and reduce budgets as savings come in, is to use finance to monitor and maintain the savings.

Even Best Practice models are occasionally challenged by Strategic Sourcing's Step 6, translating gains into management's language and publicizing successes. Purchasing executives are unaccustomed to working in the corporate public relations realm, but at this stage, that is exactly what must be done. When the chief procurement officer's contributions to corporate profitability are understood, management always wants more. The challenge is to publicize the good results and consolidate the power base.

Taking Best Practices into the Supply Base

We dedicated an entire chapter to developing a stronger supply base by working with suppliers because we know developing a stronger supply base guarantees big returns fast. In Chapter 4, "Working with Suppliers," we reviewed the range of possible partnering and developmental approaches, starting with the premise that it takes time and money to work with suppliers. Supplier development has guaranteed payback—the only question is which areas should be addressed for the biggest returns.

Honda of America is the most frequently cited model of supplier development. Starting with Japanese manufacturing and supply chain ideas, the Marysville complex eventually built a local supply network that demonstrates how much can be achieved in less than five years. Results for Honda's BP supplier development work are solid and consistently high in all key areas, including quality, cycle time, productivity, inventory, and downtime.

Delphi Corporation is a second-tier supplier to the Big Three and others with first-tier ideas. Delphi's lean operations have won the Shingo Award twenty times, and the company's procurement group is implementing Best Practices. Delphi's manufacturing system includes value stream mapping to identify waste and smooth flows, and it is a key contributor to integration and stronger suppliers.

We discussed an additional approach that traditional supply chains have not used—enterprise mapping and network optimization using smart software. Most supply networks have grown globally to satisfy delivery requirements to factories, but they may not offer the best logistics, cost, or market growth solutions. Software technology offers a unique leapfrog solution, however. Schneider National, North America's largest privately held truckload carrier and one of the world's best transport and logistics providers, illustrates how to construct and improve the best distribution networks. The payback includes better collaboration, faster throughput, and lower overall costs.

Every method of planning, processing, moving, and shipping materials has a value placed on it. Every move costs money. Our approach to the payback, therefore, requires buyers and planners to think like commodity traders that live minute to minute with price shifts. A missed opportunity, or a premature trade, can cost millions; the same watchful eye is what takes ordinary purchasing performance to the level of successful commodity markets. In fact,

Motorola's chief procurement officer and IBM veteran Theresa Metty takes a commodity approach to the company's innovative cellular market. Metty knows that her buyers are capable of finding big savings, and by combining purchasing that resembles commodity trading, and strong market intelligence supported by excellent suppliers, she is realizing big paybacks.

Finally, working with suppliers does not begin when prototypes are released to production. Tooling, process selection, component specification, and dropping component prices are all influenced early in the development stage by engineering. When purchasing buyers engage the process as well, as they do at Honda, Lucent, IBM, and other leaders, the results are even bigger.

Overall, working with suppliers starts with an easy progression and works toward tougher challenges around product pricing and acquiring the best and most competitive technologies. Companies that think that working with suppliers stops with supplier development and fixing the process are missing most of The Incredible Payback potential of the extended supply chain.

We know what the basic requirements are for achieving good paybacks, and we've covered an approximate time frame for setting the building blocks in place. But every operation is different, with different people, organizational structure, and systems. No one supply management group will be starting out at the same place as another, and that's why Chapter 5 contains so many examples drawn from Honda, the 10X Project, and a slew of fresh and powerful technology solutions.

Your operation may need more training, or better spend and cost data, or most likely, more powerful and comprehensive computer systems. It is important to start out with a checklist or a map of which capabilities are most important to your particular challenge, and which ones will yield the biggest paybacks. We urge companies not to waste valuable energy or money on an attractive, but low yield approach.

Putting It All Together

The Honda of America purchasing group has been cited by *Purchasing* magazine with its Medal of Excellence Award, as well as other studies that place Honda in the top three procurement groups. The Honda solution is a unique one that no other enterprise could exactly replicate, but because its supplier development, quality training, spend management, and kaizen work is so outstanding, benchmarkers should pick and choose from Honda's accelerated supply network experience and adapt it for their own challenges. First, Honda supplier development BP methods are proven and simple approaches to guaranteed process and inventory improvement. Consult *Powered by Honda* for a detailed guide to Honda BP (kaizen).

Delphi is another example of supply chain transformation, from a division completely controlled by GM to an established and independent supply chain covering new industries—medical and aerospace—as well as automotive. Delphi's supply management and profitability objectives have changed as well, and in a short time the company has learned from Honda and Toyota and constructed its own model to move forward. The key to Delphi's big plans is its cost management expertise, a new area filled with opportunity.

Among the invaluable tools we recommend for pulling projects and all their details together is a method always used by Honda and its suppliers: the A-3 report. This simple approach to planning and executing all work offers a great starting point for purchasing project leaders and suppliers to set goals and track completion. It is a time saver as team members take on increasingly complicated work, and it facilitates communications and alignment. Every Honda supplier is familiar with this document, and every purchasing planner or supplier development engineer uses it as the starting point and summary sheet for each improvement project.

Communications—*Get the Word Out!*

Finally, every successful implementation deserves rave notices. Awards like the Purchasing Medal of Excellence and the Shingo Award are good for the winners as well as their suppliers, and they reinforce all the hard work change-makers and team members take on.

Delphi, for example, has learned valuable technical lessons about becoming leaner from Toyota and Honda, but education and communication work hand in hand to support change. Delphi's supply management group has developed its own unique approach to good communications; internally, employees continue to learn the value of the supply chain's contribution and the leverage it maintains on profits. Externally, the company occupies a unique position of visibility as a first-tier supplier. Any supply group beginning its transformation should develop and include a positive communications strategy in its change plan, one that is designed to touch internal areas such as engineering and new products and externally, its suppliers.

Guaranteeing the Payback on Your Investment

"Let the data lead you."

—Dorian Shainin, Shewhart Award Winner

Metrics started this journey when the numbers describing key procurement practices opened up new possibilities for big paybacks. Now, statistics on quality and delivery performance should be easily obtained. These are the numbers that keep the everyday operation on track. Information on Spend Management and other Best Practices, the bigger payback contributors, might appear, however, with more difficulty. Nevertheless, every aspect of The Incredible Payback, even reviewing alignment on soft issues like customer culture, is measurable and important for analysis. Any time spent on establishing cost data will be paid back in more than one form—in cost savings, as well as competitive advantage.

However your organization decides to prioritize savings goals and projects, the numbers must always drive the process and inform participants as well as observers. Making clear links between a project's anticipated payoffs and income statement contributions is very important and will take the entire supply management group into a higher, more strategic operating level.

The Best Practice giants use purchasing spend numbers to drive total corporate strategies. They know that a slight change up or down in prices or total spend, or a performance problem in the supply base—from inventory accumulation to new product shortages—can easily fracture even the best financial plans.

We've reviewed Best Practice examples and good payback models that should allow any traditional operation to achieve payback in less than one year. When your organization begins the process, expect to be surprised by the absolute simplicity of the problem—finding opportunities, consolidating, and reducing spend is not magic, but it is a gold mine of challenges and opportunities.

A journey begins with one step—we urge you to take it.

An Epilogue from Dave Nelson

Make Chance Your Opportunity

Sometimes, just when we think we have the answer, something happens to change our minds.

In 1966 I was pretty sure about the path I was on. I was a metals engineer headed up the production ladder. But then a chance—an opportunity—changed my life forever.

I was working in Lafayette, Indiana, my hometown, at the Ross Gear Division of TRW. I had been there nine years in manufacturing and quality control, with seventy-six people reporting to me, which was a handful.

Chance walked into my plant one Friday afternoon when I literally bumped into the CEO in the men's room. "Dave," he said, "I've been wanting to talk with you. Have you ever thought of going into purchasing?" "No," I told him. I had never thought about it. But he was ready for my answer, "Well, what do you think? Do you think you'd like it?"

For a nanosecond I thought of telling the truth. But instead, I fortuitously told him a little lie: "Yes," I said, "I think I *would* like purchasing."

To that, he smiled and said, "Good, report to purchasing Monday morning!"

That chance, and the little white lie, thirty-seven years ago became a big opportunity, one that changed my life. Many years have passed since then, and I have gained some additional experience in my profession. I've logged 6 million miles, had some successes, and even a few roadblocks. I've usually had a vision of what I want and where I want to go. Sometimes I've even had a plan.

But everything good that's happened to me has happened not just because I had a plan, but because I took a chance. I've rerouted my road map and periodically asked myself, "What's next?"—and I made chance my opportunity.

Make Chance Your Opportunity

Po Bronson, a former bond trader turned writer, gathered life stories of more than nine hundred people and then spent time with seventy of them. He asked each one how he or she had answered the question: "What should I do with my life?" Bronson concluded that almost everyone interviewed found his or her calling only after great difficulty:

❏   A catfish farmer used to be an investment banker.
❏   A truck driver used to be an entertainment lawyer.
❏   A police officer had a Harvard MBA.

Bronson believes that the answer to the question "What should I do with my life" doesn't usually strike like a lightning bolt, but most of the time in merely a small voice or faint urge.

If Bronson is right—and if our true calling usually reveals itself in just a whisper—how can we possibly make it a reality? My answer is to keep your ears—and your options—open, listening for the whisper and making chance your opportunity. As I became more involved in purchasing management, I realized I needed to know more about my new profession.

For me, that meant a lot more work and preparation than luck. So in 1967 I took two important steps. First, I joined the predecessor of the Institute for Supply Management, which was called the National Association of Purchasing Agents (NAPA). Meetings were held at my old school, Purdue University, in Lafayette.

Second, through NAPA, I took my first certification course, The Fundamentals of Purchasing.

This was not an easy course. Two of us drove 130 miles round-trip every week for ten weeks back and forth to Indianapolis. The instructor was Richard Bothel, a vice president of purchasing at Ford's steering gear operation in Indianapolis. Richard Bothel's classes, and the fact that a senior member of the profession took to time to teach the rest of us, made a strong and lasting impression on me. This fundamentals course, and so many others that followed, reinforced the idea that opportunities come not to those who wait but to those who prepare. I call it leveling up.

Leveling Up

Preparation for opportunity disguised as chance means learning everything about a chosen profession: the employer's goals, the market position, the competition, and every other issue and concern for the top brass. However, most of us don't start our careers with a laminated road map, and few of us don't encounter roadblocks and detours.

Near the end of his life, George Bernard Shaw was asked if he could start over as someone else, who would he want to be. Although Shaw had mingled with kings, millionaires, authors, scoundrels, artists, teachers, and celebrities from all over the world, his response was stunning: "I would choose to be the George Bernard Shaw who *could* have been—but who never was."

Most of us never fully reach our potential, but a few may come close. In my life, I have come to believe that the ones who come the closest have the following six things in common:

1. They start by honing their skills and building experience.
2. They learn from others and pass it on—at work, at home, and in their communities.
3. They study their employers so they can understand what is important to the organization's overall success—and they learn to speak the language of management.
4. They have a vision, but they are not afraid to change plans when chance provides them with an opportunity.
5. They set high standards. Excellence is a habit for them.
6. They pay attention to relationships, putting a high value on ethical behavior and trust.

One day, that same TRW CEO called me about a problem he had with one of our bearing distributors. "With all of our other distributors, we have about a 14 to 15 percent market share. But with Detroit Ball Bearing, we have only about half that. I need you to find out why and see if you can fix it."

Not long thereafter, I attended a meeting with several distributors, including the grandson of the founder of Detroit Ball Bearing, our distributor challenge. TRW was looking for two representatives—one from TRW and one from a distributor—to fly to Clarkston College in New York and present two scholarships. At the distributors' meeting, there was a call for volunteers. Amazingly, the founder's grandson's hand was the first to go up. And when I saw *his* hand go up, mine went up immediately too!

We flew into Montreal and rented a car for the drive to Clarkston. As we drove, I found an opportunity to ask about TRW's relationship with Detroit Ball Bearing. "You know, everywhere else we have about a 14 to 15 percent market share, but with Detroit, we have only about half that. My CEO asked me to find out why," I said.

The grandson smiled and told this story. "My grandfather founded Detroit Ball Bearing before the Depression, and the company did well and made a lot of money. But then hard times came, and like a lot of businessmen, my grandfather finally reached the point where he couldn't make payroll. So he began calling his accounts one by one to tell them he was going out of business.

"One of Granddad's calls was to a competitor of yours, and as he started to tell his story, the man at the other end stopped him cold. 'This is too important to discuss on the telephone. I want you to come to New York so we can talk about this face to face.'

"So grandfather boarded a train for New York. He went immediately to the man's office and started to explain why it was necessary to close his doors, but the man stopped him midsentence. He went to the safe and pulled out two money belts. 'Your company is too important to both of us to close it down. We need you to be our sales arm. This is all I can give you, but maybe it will help.'

"In fact, that money got my grandfather through the Depression, and he didn't have to shut the doors.

"And so, the reason TRW only has a 7 percent share with my company today is because since the Great Depression, your competitor has never done anything to hurt the relationship established with my grandfather."

Well, there wasn't much that I could say after that story. And when I went back to TRW and told my CEO the story, he never said another word about it either. He well understood the power of relationships based on mutual commitment, trust, and respect.

Sometimes little opportunities become big chances to build relationships, to form new ones, and to be a better person or a better partner. But I think that these chances don't come every day, and sometimes they are indeed just a whisper. You have to be prepared and listen carefully to hear them when they call.

Good luck on all your journeys!

—Dave Nelson

Index

About the Authors

Dave Nelson is vice president of global supply management at Delphi Corporation, a world leader in mobile electronics and transportation components and systems technology. He is also a member of the Delphi Strategy Board, the company's top policy-making group. Additionally, Nelson serves as the executive champion for Delphi's Global Supply Management Task Team.

From 1957 to 1987, Nelson worked for TRW Inc. in various manufacturing, quality control metallurgy, materials, sales, and marketing positions, in addition to purchasing.

Next, Nelson served for ten years as a corporate officer of Honda of America Manufacturing in Marysville, Ohio, as vice president of purchasing and later as senior vice president of purchasing and corporate affairs. He was promoted to the board of directors of Honda of America Manufacturing in 1997. During his tenure at Honda he saw the company's purchasing division grow from 100 to 400 associates and North American purchases increase from $600 million to $6 billion. Honda of America was the 1995 recipient of the Medal of Professional Excellence from *Purchasing* magazine.

After Nelson's time at Honda, he served as vice president of worldwide supply management at Deere & Company in Moline,

Illinois, for four years. Under his direction, Deere became known for implementing world-class supply management processes and best practices. In 2001, those efforts were recognized when *Purchasing* magazine awarded Deere the Medal of Professional Excellence, the purchasing industry's highest award. Nelson joined Delphi and was named to his current position in February 2002.

Nelson has long been involved in advancing the purchasing and supply management profession and holds a Certified Purchasing Manager certification. He is chair emeritus of the Institute of Supply Management (formerly the National Association of Purchasing Management), sits on the boards of CAPS Research, the National Minority Supplier Development Council, and the Purchasing Round Table, and is a member of National Initiative of Supply Chain Integration, Ltd. He is also the chairman of the OESA Chief Purchasing Officer's Council.

Nelson is a founding member of the National Initiative of Supply Chain Integration, Ltd., a public/private partnership devoted to developing and enhancing manufacturing supply chains. He also serves on the board of directors of the Purchasing Round Table.

Nelson coauthored *Powered by Honda* and *The Purchasing Machine*, a book on managing supply chains at ten top companies.

Patricia E. Moody is a veteran management consultant and writer with about thirty years of industry, consulting, and teaching experience, and a client list that includes Fortune 500 industry leaders British Petroleum, Respironics, Cisco Systems, Solectron, Motorola, and Johnson & Johnson. During the Tylenol poisoning crisis, she developed a response strategy and a system that is credited with saving the company.

Named by *Fortune* magazine "One of Ten Pioneering Women in Manufacturing," she was featured on CNN's *21st Century with Bernard Shaw*. She has published eleven business books, including *Powered by Honda, The Kaizen Blitz, The Technology Machine, The Purchasing Machine,* and *The Perfect Engine.* The former editor of the Association for Manufacturing Excellence's *Target* magazine, she has authored dozens of business features, and has been quoted and reviewed in *Fortune, Sloan Management Review, Purchasing* magazine, *Supply Strategy, Purchasing Today, Managing Automation, Target, Quality Digest, IMC Journal, The Fabricator, Computerworld,* and *Metallux News,* among others. She serves on the editorial boards of ISM's *Inside Supply Management,* and *The Sloan Management Review.*

She can be reached at PEMoody@aol.com.

Jonathan R. Stegner is general director, Delphi Global Supply Management, for Delphi Corporation and an expert supply management strategist and implementer with more than 25 years of delivering bottom-line results.

Stegner joined Delphi in 2001 as one of the primary architects of the company's global supply management lean-transformation strategy. This highly integrated plan combines the power of strategic sourcing, cost management, lean supplier development engineering, new model flawless launch, quality, supplier relationships, systems, people development, and change management. The approach also reflects Stegner's deep understanding of the practical steps and processes required to achieve benchmark levels of competitiveness.

Stegner's Delphi responsibilities include lean supplier development engineering, supplier quality, and strategic sourcing for indirect material and machinery and equipment. He leads global supply management financial controls; policy, procedures, and processes; minority supplier development; people development; and communication.

Prior to joining Delphi, Stegner was director, supply management strategic sourcing, for Deere & Company. In that role he was responsible for development and implementation of common processes for strategic sourcing, supplier development and logistics, and implementation of global common systems.

As Honda's manager of purchasing, planning, and administration, he participated in many initiatives regarded as integral to the rise of Honda's purchasing division to benchmark status. He also was director of purchasing for Bush Industries, Inc., and manager of purchasing at TRW.

Stegner is a frequent contributor to *Purchasing* magazine, *iSource* and other publications. He is also coauthor of *The Purchasing Machine: How the Top Ten Companies Use Best Practices to Manage Their Supply Chains.*

Stegner is a native of Olean, New York, and a graduate of St. Bonaventure University, where he earned a bachelor's degree in economics in 1976 and a master's of business administration in 1983. He is an active member of the Institute for Supply Management, formerly known as the National Association for Purchasing Management. He lives in Clarkston, Michigan.